SOLOMON

TEMPLE

by
W. W. FEREDAY

JOHN RITCHIE LTD.
PUBLISHERS OF CHRISTIAN LITERATURE
40 BEANSBURN, KILMARNOCK KA3 1RH

Solomon and His Temple

ISBN 0-946351 36 8

Copyright © 1993 by John Ritchie Ltd.
40 Beansburn, Kilmarnock, Scotland.

Printed by Bell & Bain Ltd., Glasgow.

Foreword

READING of a biographical character is always interesting, and it is frequently profitable. But the Spirit of God, when recording the life-stories of men, differs from all others in the line that He pursues. Human biographers aim at presenting the commendable side of the characters with which they deal, and they either draw a veil over their ugly features, or touch them lightly or apologetically. But the Spirit of God tells us the whole truth about the men whose lives He is pleased to record. It could not be otherwise. The Bible is the revelation of God Himself — all that He is is told out there; and the same Book must needs also show us man as he really is. The goodness of God and the badness of man are there presented side by side for our instruction and blessing.

Critics have often found fault with the Bible for its frank exposures of human evil. But its fearlessness in this particular is one of the many proofs of its divine origin, and how thankful should we be to have the whole truth laid before us!

The Spirit of God has laid special emphasis upon the foibles of Simon Peter. We know his vagaries better than those of any of his companions. Indeed, if all the passages which present him to us unfavourably were eliminated from the Bible story, we should know very little of this singular servant of our Lord Jesus. There is doubtless divine design in this. The Spirit knew (though His inspired penman did not) the use that would be made of Peter's name at a later date, and so has taken pains to show us that the Apostle was not infallible, whatever his pretended successors may claim to be.

On the same principle the Spirit has carefully noted certain occasions when Mary, the mother of our Lord, asked favours of Him, and was refused (John 2. 10; Matt. 12. 48), while omitting altogether the many occasions which must have occurred when He did for her what she desired. So all-wise is our God!

Preface to 2nd Edition

W.W. Fereday was born in England in 1863, was saved at 16 and almost immediately started to preach. He spent the whole of his life in the study and exposition of the Scripture of Truth and travelled extensively and spent a considerable time in Scotland and the continent of Europe. He was a faithful expositor of the Word of God. He knew no fear and never compromised for one moment, but one could not help but love him.

He lived for many years in Rothesay, Scotland, and the last five years of his life at Machermore Eventide Home, Scotland, from where he went to be with the Lord at the age of 96. He was the last of a worthy kind — John Nelson Darby, William Kelly, William Woldridge Fereday. Brother Fereday always had two life size portraits of these two revered men of God in his large study; he knew them both personally and they were guides to him in his early formative years.

Many lovers of the Scriptures have spent long hours immersing themselves in the writings of J.N. Darby and have found them at first reading almost beyond understanding. However, after a further reading, the truth conveyed gradually shone through and one could grasp the writer's meaning and then would gladly acknowledge that what he wrote was undoubtedly laborious; he wandered into many unnecessary by-paths. An enormous number of pages had to be read in order to obtain a small portion of truth but, we hasten to add, a very sweet portion.

However W.W. Fereday was different. Precise, accurate, lucid, brief; he was as succinct in his written ministry as in his public addresses. One of his favourite expressions was "I do not give lectures, I state facts". He never wasted a word, wrote in the briefest possible way, taught the same truths as J.N.D. and W.K. but in a language that was simple, interesting, and often thrilling; in fact just in the form that young Christians will appreciate today.

John Ritchie Limited have done a great service to the Lord's people in republishing these books in paperback. We are sure God will use them in blessing to this present generation.

A.M.S. Gooding

Preface

THE following pages were written by an aged pilgrim upon a sick-bed in intervals of comparative freedom from pain. The reader who may discover blunders and deficiencies will therefore please regard them with that gracious pitifulness which is always delightful in the children of God; and like the careful fishermen of Matthew 13.48 he will put "the good into vessels and cast the bad away."

The days of Solomon were unique in the history of Israel and of the world; and the house that he built unto the name of Jehovah was also unique. It was all a bright foreshadowing of days of glory and blessing yet to be brought in by the Lord Jesus. The nations of the world will then cease to strive, and will dwell peacefully under His righteous sway, and the Temple in Jerusalem will be sought unto from the ends of the earth because Jehovah is there.

"Amen. Come, Lord Jesus" (Rev. 22.20).

Solomon and His Temple

Contents

Kingship in Israel

THE commanding theme of Holy Scripture-of Scripture in its every part, is Christ. He is everything to God, and His Spirit delights to make known to us the glories of His person, the perfection of His work, and the Father's eternal counsels respecting Him. Our principal interest in Solomon lies in the fact that he was a foreshadow of Christ. The peace of his reign, his righteous and wise administration, the prosperity of the people, and the homage of all the kings round about, all suggest conditions that will be true on a larger and more glorious scale when God's true Anointed sits upon His holy hill of Zion (Psalm 2.6). Solomon's administration, alas, finished badly, due to his own unfaithfulness. Far otherwise will it be with Christ. At the end of His long reign, "He will deliver up the kingdom to Him who is God and Father, when He shall have put down all rule and all authority and power.... Then shall the Son Himself be subject unto Him that put all things under Him, that God may be all in all" (1 Cor. 15.24, 28). He who was faithful when here in poverty and humiliation will also be faithful in the day of His kingdom exaltation.

When Solomon was born his father named him Solomon, which means "Peaceable" (2 Sam. 12.24). Jehovah thus named him before his birth (1 Chron. 22.9). But when he was born He sent Nathan the prophet to David with a second name for the child - Jedidiah, which means "beloved of Jehovah" (2 Sam. 12.25). It is added, "Jehovah loved him." Another has remarked, "Nathan, with a marked reference to the meaning of the King's own name (David = the darling, the beloved one), calls the infant Jedidiah (Jedid-yah), that is, the darling of the Lord." Loved by God; chosen by God; preferred by Him above all others for the throne-what an expressive type of our blessed Lord! He is God's true beloved (Isa. 42.1), who in His due time "will speak peace to the nations, and His dominion shall be from sea to sea, and from the river to the ends of the earth" (Zech. 9.10).

The inspired historian - Moses, we doubt not - tells us in Genesis 36.31 that "kings reigned in the land of Edom before there reigned any king over the children of Israel." He who wrote the Chronicles after the return of the remnant from the Babylonian captivity repeats the statement (1 Chron. 1.43). Edom as a people was very nearly related to Israel; but although not God's chosen for supremacy in the earth Edom had kings (an honour, as men judge) before Israel. Kings developed rapidly after the break-up of the human family into nations. Nimrod came first as founder of the dominion of Babylon (Gen. 10.8-10); Egypt comes next in the sacred record as ruled by a king (Gen. 12.15); and in Genesis xiv. we read of two confederacies of kings at war with each other. Unhappy foreshadow of worse things to come!

But why was Israel so long without a monarch? God certainly spoke of a king for the nation while they were still in the wilderness, and gave instructions and warnings as to his conduct. He must not multiply horses, nor wives, nor silver and gold; but he must write out for himself a copy of the law, which he was to read all the days of his life that all might be well (Deut. 17.14-20). Balaam, when constrained by the Spirit of God to say against his will good things about the people he hated, declared: "Jehovah his God is with him, and the shout of a king is among them." Further, "His king shall be higher than Agag, and his kingdom shall be exalted" (Num. 23.21; 24.7). Hannah in her prophetic song was led to say, "Jehovah shall judge the ends of the earth; and He shall give strength unto His king, and exalt the horn of His anointed" (1 Sam. 2.10).

Why, then, was Israel several centuries in the land of promise before kingship was established? For the very blessed reason, if the people could have appreciated it, Jehovah was their king. It was their glory to be living under a theocracy. Jehovah Himself personally directed their affairs. No nation has ever been thus honoured, and no nation will ever have such an honour until the seventh trumpet is sounded in Heaven, and great voices say, "The Kingdom of the world of our Lord and of His Christ is come, and He shall reign to the ages of ages" (Rev. 11.15; J.N.D.). Then all the nations (not Israel only) will come under direct divine rule. This will be the final solution of all earth's difficulties and sorrows.

Israel, as the people of Jehovah's gracious choice, was meant to be different in every respect to all others, and to be Jehovah's witness to them. Balaam, in his first utterance said, "Lo, it is a people that shall dwell alone, and shall not be reckoned amongst the nations" (Num. 23.9). It was therefore deplorable when the people demanded of Samuel, "Make us a king to judge us like all the nations" (1 Sam. 8.5).

Let us pause here and take account of ourselves. The Church is a company divinely called out and separated from the world. It is the body of the absent Christ (here to represent Him), and the house of God, the Assembly of the living God (Acts 15.14; 1 Cor. 12.13; 1 Tim. 3.15). Do we appreciate the inestimable honour and privilege of being a people separated to God? The history of the Church since the days of the Apostles reveals the grossest unfaithfulness in this respect. The Church and the world have long been friends, to the Lord's dishonour, and to the spiritual injury of the saints. Further, the Church has been distinguished from the beginning as having its Head in Heaven, with the Holy Spirit dwelling on earth to act for Him. With respect to these great realities we have also been long unfaithful. Faith in the invisible Head in Heaven, and in the invisible Spirit on earth has lapsed; hence the hordes of Popes, Bishops, clergy, chairmen, etc. The Church, like Israel before her, has wished to be "like all the nations." It is not even yet too late for some at least to recover themselves, and return repentantly to the right ways of God.

Israel's wilful descent from the high level upon which Jehovah in His grace placed them at the beginning of their national history has been recorded as instruction for us today (Rom. 15.4). For as surely as the people of Israel were divinely intended to be the aristocracy of the earth, those who are now being blessed and who compose the Church are the aristocracy of the universe. Our conduct should be consistent with our dignity.

Samuel felt deeply the people's demand for a king "like all the nations," but Jehovah said to His servant, "Hearken unto the voice of the people in all that they say unto thee: for they have not rejected thee, but they have rejected Me, that I should not reign over them" (1 Sam. 8.7). The theocracy was thus at an end until the day of the Lord Jesus.

The Spirit's words through Balaam and Hannah make it certain that Jehovah always had it in His mind to give Israel a king. Ultimately the king of His choice is Christ, but it was His intention that men typical of Him should occupy the throne meantime. Both David and Solomon, each in his own way, typify Him. But the impatience of the people could not wait for God to act; they would have a king forthwith. God knew where to find the sort of man that they wanted; thus Saul was anointed first king of Israel with disastrous consequences for all concerned.

Scripture numerals are instructive. Forty is the number of full trial (Psalm 95.10; Matt. 4.2). For forty years Saul reigned. The trial ended with the dead bodies of the king and his sons nailed to the wall of Bethshan by the insolent foe, and the people scattered as sheep having no shepherd (1 Sam. 31.). What confidence dare we have in flesh?

David and Solomon

THE youthful Solomon had not to wait until the death of his father to sit upon his throne. "When David was old and full of days, he made Solomon his son king over Israel" (1 Chron. 23.1). The usurpation of Adonijah, not mentioned in the Book of Chronicles, led to a second enthronement. "They made Solomon the son of David king the second time, and anointed him unto Jehovah to be the chief governor." At this point David's throne is called "The throne of Jehovah" (1 Chron. 29.22-23). Title of exaltation indeed, and acknowledged by the Queen of Sheba on the occasion of her visit (2 Chron. 9.8). David's throne has a place in the ways of God that no other has ever had, or can have. It is the centre of divine administration for the earth, and can only be filled in perfection by the Lord Jesus. It was a sad day for all the nations as well as for Israel when Jehovah in righteousness was constrained to "make his glory to cease, and cast his throne down to the ground" (Psalm 89.44). Then commenced "the times of the Gentiles" (Luke 21.24).

The enthronement of Solomon while David yet lived meant that for the time being both reigned together. Thus we have a twofold picture of Christ. David typifies Him as the man of war, and Solomon as the man of peace. Our Lord at His appearing will fulfil the David type in His warrior judgments; and afterwards He will fulfil the Solomon type in His sessional judgments. The white horse is the symbol of the one and the throne is the symbol of the other.

Revelation 19.11-21 gives us a vivid description of our Lord coming forth from heaven in His David character. The white horse is the symbol of victorious power, contrast to the ass's colt upon which He rode in the day of His lowly grace (Mark 11.7). His name is Faithful and True. What He was in testimony for God He will also be in the execution of His judgments. Let all deniers of the judgment of God beware! "In righteousness He doth judge and make war". Here at last we have an unquestionably "righteous war." Through dreary ages men have striven to keep the Man of God's choice out of His rights. "Let us seize upon His inheritance" (Matt. 21.38). "The inheritance shall be ours" (Mark 12.7). Such has been the language of creature-arrogance, and God has borne with it! The King's eyes are a "flame of fire" - holy discernment in wrath. "On His head are many diadems." Satan has seven (Rev. 12.3); and the Beast ten (Rev. 13.1). The King of Kings and Lord of Lords has "many" for His glory is without limit. Armies follow Him, also riding "upon white horses, clothed in fine linen, white and clean." These are the glorified saints, previously "caught up" at His descent into the air (1 Thess. 4.15-17). There is no suggestion of mercy in the terrible vision of Revelation 19. "Out of His mouth goeth a sharp sword, that with it He should smite the nations: and He treadeth the winepress of the fierceness of the wrath of Almighty God." The fowls of the heavens are angelically summoned to the greatest feast yet known. Kings, captains, mighty men, horses, etc., go down at the word of Him who rides the white horse. The vast hosts of the Roman group of Powers will be impotent before Him, and their leaders, the Beast and the False Prophet will be "cast alive into a lake of fire burning with brimstone."

Isaiah 63.1-6 describes another terrible incident in our Lord's warrior judgments. He comes up from Edom with garments dyed with the blood of the enemies of His redeemed (i.e. Israel). These are the Northern and Eastern Powers who will over-run God's land in the last crisis (Zech. 14.1-3). The groups of Revelation 19 and Isaiah 63 are hostile to each other, each seeking world-supremacy; but all are equally opposed to the Christ of God, and would frustrate, if they could, the accomplishment of the divine counsels concerning Him. But their schemes are laughable to the Almighty! (Psalm 2.4).

There are other fearful incidents in the judgment of the

"Quick" at the Lord's appearing upon which we will not dwell. Ezekiel 38. and 39. speaks of the overthrow of the hordes of Russia and her many Allies (or satellites); Isaiah 11.14 tells of the judgment of Edom, Moab, and Ammon by Jewish instrumentality, and the following Scriptures suggest much more activity of this painful character - Micah 4.13; 5.8; Ezekiel 25.14; Zechariah 9.13; 14.14; Psalm 149.6-9. All these prophecies bring home to us the solemn meaning of our Lord's words, "Those mine enemies, which would not that I should reign over them, bring them hither, and slay them before Me" (Luke 19.27).

David having subdued all the enemies of Israel round about, bequeathed to Solomon a peaceful throne. Only one military incident is recorded. "Solomon went to Hamath-zobah, and prevailed against it" (2 Chron. 8.3). Then profound peace during the remainder of his forty years' reign. "Solomon reigned over all kingdoms from the river (Euphrates) unto the land of the Philistines, and unto the border of Egypt; they brought presents and served Solomon all the days of his life" (1 Kings 4.21). But Solomon was no believer in disarmament! It is twice repeated, "Solomon gathered together chariots and horsemen: and he had a thousand and four hundred chariots, and twelve thousand horsemen, whom he bestowed in the cities for chariots, and with the king at Jerusalem" (1 Kings 10.26; 2 Chron. 1.14). Truly every type fails! When He who is "greater than Solomon" reigns in Jerusalem, men "shall beat their swords into ploughshares, and their spears into pruning hooks: nation shall not lift up sword against nation, neither shall they learn war any more" (Isa. 2.4). His presence will cause "the name of the city from that day to be Jehovah Shammah-Jehovah is there" (Ezek. 48.35). "I, saith Jehovah, will be unto her a wall of fire round about, and will be the glory in the midst of her" (Zech. 2.5).

At this point it would be a delight to transcribe the whole of Psalm 72. but we refrain. In days of universal distress such as our own, it is refreshing to the spirit to read that Psalm. David began it as a prayer for Solomon, but the Spirit of God soon led him far beyond his immediate successor to the One who will bring all blessing in, and establish it upon immutable foundations. David begins with righteousness (in both king and subordinate rulers), and in his seventh verse he arrives at peace - "abundance of peace as long as the moon endureth." Justice for all; every oppressor broken in pieces; all enemies subjugated; kings from afar bowing low at the feet of David's greater Son; widespread prosperity; city life purified and made healthy; and men everywhere calling Him blessed - these are the themes of which the Psalmist wrote with joy. We need not wonder that he turned to praise. "Blessed be Jehovah God, the God of Israel, Who only doeth wondrous things. And blessed be His glorious name for ever: and let the whole earth be filled with His glory: Amen and Amen. The prayers of David the Son of Jesse are ended." This does not mean that David never prayed after he wrote Psalm 72. What is meant is that from his standpoint as a saint with an earthly calling he could ask nothing beyond an earth filled with righteousness, peace, and glory under the rule of the Man of God's pleasure. Heavenly saints look for much more - a "vast universe of bliss," of which Christ will be the "Centre and the Sun."

David's last words (2 Sam. 23.1-7) are in subdued tone. He could see in prophetic vision a just king ruling in the fear of God, who should be "as the light of the morning, when the sun riseth, a morning without clouds." But that king is not Solomon, but Christ. The dying king added, "Although my house be not so with God: yet He hath made with me an everlasting covenant, ordered in all things and sure: for this is all my salvation, and all my desire, although He make it not to grow." Solomon's hand was not steady enough to hold the full cup of blessing which God placed therein, and for three thousand years Israel and all nations have suffered through his unfaithfulness.

Adonjah's Usurpation

THE first mention of Jerusalem in the Word of God brings before us a delightful type of Christ in the person of Melchizedek, King of righteousness and King of peace (Gen. 14.18-20; Heb. 7.1). The second mention of Jerusalem is startling by its contrast. Joshua found Adonizedek reigning there, and determined to hold the city in defiance of Jehovah's purpose for His people (Josh. 10.1). This king suggests the Antichrist who will defy the Lamb at His appearing. Adonizedek perished ignominiously; with his confederate kings he was hanged. The Antichrist (described in the Apocalypse as "the false prophet") will be consigned with his partner in iniquity, the ten-horned Beast, to the lake of fire a thousand years before even Satan is sent there (Rev. 19.20).

The revelation of a divine purpose arouses the opposition of the Devil, and he labours forthwith to frustrate the accomplishment of it. 1 Chronicles 22. describes an important gathering in Jerusalem when David made it known that Solomon, although one of his youngest sons, was Jehovah's choice for the throne. He forthwith charged him to build a house for God (how delighted would David have been to have built it himself!); and he also charged all the princes of Israel to help Solomon his son (1 Chron. 22.17). The young man was then solemnly enthroned.

It was after this, and thus in full knowledge of the purpose of God, that "Adonijah the son of Haggith exalted himself, saying, I will be king," and in his vanity "prepared him chariots and horsemen, and fifty men to run before him" (1 Kings 1.5). As surely as Solomon prefigures Christ, Adonijah prefigures the Antichrist. Mark the fatal words, "I will." In Isaiah 14.13-14 we hear Lucifer saying five times, "I will." Here we have the very essence of sin. 1 John 3.4, correctly translated, teaches us that "sin is lawlessness." Lawlessness is self-will. James tells us that we should always say, "if the Lord will. . . we shall do this or that" (James 4.15). Self-will has been the undoing of the human race, and its full evil is not yet developed.

All who have been born of the Spirit should abhor the restlessness of flesh in every form, and find delight in doing the will of God. The Man Christ is our perfect example of will-lessness. When He came into the world He said, "I delight to do Thy will, O my God" (Psalm 40.8); in the night of His sorrow He desired only the will of the Father to be done (Matt. 26.39); and in the midst of His service He told the people around Him, "I came down from heaven, not to do mine own will, but the will of Him that sent me" (John 6.38). Every bit of self-will in which we indulge savours not of Christ, but of Antichrist!

Adonijah was apparently a "spoilt child." The Holy Spirit says, "His father had not displeased him at any time in saying, Why hast thou done so? and he was also a very goodly man" (1 Kings 1.6). The handsome Absalom, slightly his senior, was similarly treated by David. Good-looking children are in special danger when in the hands of foolish parents. The wise king's words in Proverbs 19.18 are true for all time: "Chasten thy son while there is hope, and let not thy soul spare for his crying." There are many broken hearts amongst God's saints due to the neglect of parental discipline; and the dishonour to the name of the Lord is still more serious, for the house of the Christian should be like unto the house of God, where the divine will alone should be done.

Adonijah's usurpation was short-lived. So will it be with the sinister figure of whom he was a pitiful foreshadow. When self-will rises to its full height, and a man proclaims himself God, judgment will fall speedily. Solomon appears to have been quiescent while the rebellion was in progress. It was his father who acted against the aggressor. In like manner the Christ of God looks with long patience at what His enemies are doing, but He will make no move until the Father gives the Word. Ultimately Adonijah perished by command of Solomon; and the man of sin will be destroyed by the "breath of the lips" of the One against whom he will exalt himself (Isa. 11.4; 2 Thess. 2.8).

Let us briefly examine a few Scriptures relative to the man in Jerusalem in the last days of whom Adonijah was a type. Daniel 11.36 speaks of him as the King - Isaiah 30.33; 57.9 also. The concluding revelation to Daniel concerning his people extends from chapter 10.12 to the end of the book. Down to chapter 11.35 everything has been already fulfilled. We read of plots and wars between successive kings of the North and of the South (Syria and Egypt), with the holy land as their battleground. There is a gap of more than twenty centuries between verses 35 and 36. From the days of the Maccabees we pass to the world's last crisis. A king is seen ruling in Palestine, whom only carelessness would confound with the kings of the North and the South, for both make war upon him.

Mark the description of this man - Palestine's last king before the establishment of the Kingdom of the Lord Jesus. "The king shall do according to his will: and he shall exalt himself, and magnify himself above every god, and shall speak marvellous (or monstrous) things against the God of gods." Every detail is the very antithesis of Christ. He did *not* His own will, but the will of His Father and God; He did *not* exalt Himself, neither did He magnify Himself. On the contrary He humbled Himself, and magnified (glorified) Him who sent Him. But He did not suit the carnal taste of Jehovah's fallen people, the man of Daniel 11.36 will be more welcome, as the Lord warned the Jews in John 5.43.

Like Adonijah, he says, " I will be king." The will of God and the well-being of the people are both alien to his thoughts. He will sweep aside every divine institution; he will seek the destruction of the pious few who venture to oppose him; and he will honour and reward the wicked (Dan. 11.37-38. His end is not mentioned in Daniel 11. The one whose "end" is referred to in the last verse is the king of the North, the powerful and implacable foe of the Jews' apostate ruler.

Now compare 2 Thessalonians 2. with Daniel 11. The language is so similar that there can be no doubt that both chapters refer to the same person. "The man of sin, the son of perdition, who opposeth and exalteth himself above all that is called God or that is worshipped: so that he sitteth in the temple of God, showing himself that he is God." The scene is clearly laid in Jerusalem, where the Jewish temple was still standing when the Epistle to the Thessalonians was written. Another temple will be seen there in the last days erected by returned Jews. It has been remarked that the Antichrist is "Adam fully developed." To Adam it was said, "You shall be as God"; Antichrist says, "I am God." In Daniel 11. we see him in Jewish connection; and in 2 Thessalonians 2. as the leader and consummation of the apostasy of Christendom. In 1 John 2.22, where alone we find the title "Antichrist", the two things are combined. "Who is the liar but he that denieth that Jesus is the Christ? He is Antichrist that denieth the Father and the Son." The Jews have from the first denied that Jesus is the Christ, and Christendom will ere long repudiate the Father and the Son. Both Jews and the multitudes who to-day "profess and call themselves Christians" will then unite in their worship of the man of sin. Solemn thought, the same city from which the truth of Christ went forth, and which has brought blessing to millions, will yet send forth the lie of the Antichrist to the ruin of all who receive it. Judicial blindness from God will settle down upon those who have had the truth within their reach, but have not loved it (2 Thess. 2.9-12).

God will know how to subdue all proud pretension in the day of His wrath. "The day of Jehovah shall be upon every one that is proud and lofty, and upon every one that is lifted up; and he shall be brought low... And the loftiness of man shall be bowed down, and the haughtiness of men shall be made low: and Jehovah alone shall be exalted in that day" (Isa. 2.12-17.) The Lord preserve us all from the Adonijah spirit of pride and self-exaltation!

The King's Dream

NEBUCHADNEZZAR went to bed one night in Babylon with the might and majesty of his Empire upon his mind, and wondering what would be the development of it. God graciously answered the poor pagan's thoughts by showing him in vision Gentile Imperialism as a whole and its ultimate destruction by the superior power of the Kingdom of God (Dan. 2). This was intended to act upon his conscience for his blessing, but no such effect was produced at that time. He was blessed later (Dan. 4.).

Solomon went to bed in Gibeon with very different thoughts exercising his mind. He had become the most exalted person on earth, head of God's chosen people, now triumphant over every foe. He felt the seriousness of his position, and the great responsibilities connected with it (he was scarcely out of his teens), and his heart turned to God. Happy would it have been for the nations throughout the centuries if rulers everywhere had felt as Solomon did that night in Gibeon (1 Kings 3.5-15).

"Jehovah appeared to Solomon in a dream by night: and God said, Ask what I shall give thee." A dream is not God's most intimate way of communicating with men, as He Himself told Aaron and Miriam in Numbers 12.6-8; but it seems certain that Solomon never knew God as his father knew Him. He lacked David's deep spiritual experience, never having suffered as he suffered. David's years of affliction gave him a knowledge of God from which we all benefit to this day as readers of his Psalms. David could have said like a later poet:

"Deep waters crossed life's pathway,
The hedge of thorns was sharp."

Such language would be foreign to Solomon. With reference to the Temple, although denied the honour of building it, it was to David that Jehovah gave all the necessary instructions, which he passed on to Solomon (1 Chron. 28.1-12). It is also noticeable that David is named in God's list of men of faith (Heb. 11.32); but not Solomon.

It was after a busy day in Gibeon when a thousand burnt-offerings were offered upon the altar that "Jehovah appeared to Solomon in a dream by night, and God said, Ask what I shall give thee." The young king's answer delighted the heart of God. First, he acknowledged His loving-kindness in giving David a son to sit upon his throne. Then he confessed his own insufficiency for the heavy responsibilities which now lay upon him. Jehovah's people were a great people, distinguished as His chosen. To guide and direct them aright in their unique relation to God was beyond his power. "I am but a little child: I know not how to go out or come in." The spirit of the little child - humble, confiding, and teachable - is becoming in us all. The Lord Jesus lays this down in Matthew 18. The concluding verses of chapter 17. give us a wonderful setting for this instruction. Peter made himself foolish with the tax-collector in Capernaum, but the Lord took occasion by it to declare the exalted position in which Peter and every other believer stands in relationship with Himself through grace. We are *sons* of the Sovereign of the universe in association with the Firstborn! (Heb. 2.10).

The believer in Jesus is thus a very dignified person, according to grace. Note the sequel. "In the same hour (the correct rendering of Matt. 18.1) came the disciples unto Jesus, saying, Who is the greatest in the kingdom of heaven? And Jesus called a little child unto Him, and set him in the midst of them, and said, Verily I say unto you, Except ye be converted and become as little children, ye shall not enter into the kingdom of heaven." Thus we have to become very small in order to enter into blessing. The next verse teaches us to continue small. "Whosoever shall humble himself as this little child, the same is greatest in the kingdom of heaven." Matthew 17.24-27 shows us the dignity of grace; Matthew 18 follows suitably, instructing us to keep small and insignificant in our own esteem. Even King Saul was little in his own sight to begin with (1 Sam. 15.17); exaltation and power drew out his inherent pride and stubbornness, to his ruin. A later king - Uzziah - walked well "till he became strong. And when he was strong, his heart was lifted up to his destruction" (2 Chron. 26.16).

Self-importance was the plague of the apostolic band. Even at the Last Supper "there was strife among them which of them should be accounted the greatest" (Luke 22.24). The coming of the Holy Spirit at Pentecost to take charge of the Assembly for Christ should have made this impossible in the new order, but flesh is ever restless. The Apostle's plain injunction in Roman 12.3 has been but little heeded: "I say, through the grace given unto me, to every man that is among you, not to think of himself more highly than he ought to think; but to think soberly, according as God hath dealt to every man the measure of faith." The vastness of the divine immensities that he ministered made Paul feel personally very small-"less than the least of all saints" (Eph. 3.8). In 1 Corinthians 14.20 we find a truly impressive appeal: "Brethren, be not children in understanding: howbeit in malice be ye babes, but in understanding be men." He had no desire that his readers should be *childish*, but he longed that they might be *childlike*. "I am among you as He that serveth," said the Lord to His self-important followers (Luke 22.27). Did He not wash their feet that very night? (John 13.).

Solomon felt that he was "but a little child"; accordingly he seized the golden opportunity divinely given to ask for "an understanding heart to judge Thy people, that I may discern between good and bad: for who is able to judge this Thy so great people?" His speech pleased Jehovah well. He might have asked for long life or riches, or the life of his enemies; instead he asked for an understanding heart that he might rule well the people of God. Our blessed Lord once said: "Seek ye first the Kingdom of God and His righteousness; and all these things shall be added unto you." On this principle Jehovah dealt with Solomon. "Behold, I have done according to thy words: lo, I have given thee a wise and an understanding heart; so that there was none like thee before thee, neither after thee shall any arise like unto thee. And I have also given thee that which thou hast not asked, both riches and honour: so that there shall not be any amongst the kings like unto thee all thy days" (1 Kings 3.11-13). This seemed to make the blessing of Israel secure, but God went on to say, "If thou wilt walk in My ways, and keep My statues." The priesthood having been in a secondary place since the breakdown of Eli and his sons, everything depended upon the fidelity of the king. The "if" to Solomon in 1 Kings 3.14 was as fatal as the "if" to Israel in Exodus 19.5, for poor flesh can never be trusted, and Solomon's failure was truly catastrophic. Blessed be God, all that has been lost by the unfaithfulness of men will be taken up by the Lord Jesus, God's faithful Second Man, on the principle of grace, and on the ground of redemption. This makes all things sure for ever.

Ere we pass from Gibeon, let us ask our own hearts what reply we would give if God were to say to us, "Ask what I shall give thee." It would be a testing moment assuredly, yea, it would be the turning-point of our lives. Elisha had a moment of testing in 1 Kings 19.19-21, and he responded well to it. He left his farm and forthwith shared the path of the persecuted prophet. Matthew was similarly tested and he abandoned a lucrative calling and followed the rejected Jesus (Matt. 9.9). What do we desire more than anything earth can give? Is it to "know Him, and the power of His resurrection, and the fellowship of His sufferings, being made conformable unto His death?" (Phil. 3.10).

Righteousness

SOLOMON is best known for his wisdom. With this divine quality his father connected righteousness. When charging his son respecting certain offenders who had hitherto been spared, David said, "Thou art a wise man, and knowest what thou oughtest to do. . . . Do therefore according to thy wisdom" (1 Kings 2.6-9). Righteousness was to be exercised with divine wisdom; thus there would be no mistakes.

Long after Solomon's day Isaiah wrote, "Behold, a king shall reign in righteousness" (chap. 32.1). That King is Christ. Isaiah's prediction follows several dreary chapters exposing the unrighteousness both of Israel's King and people. He goes on to say, "the work of righteousness shall be peace, and the effect of righteousness quietness and assurance for ever." Surely our hearts cry, "Lord Jesus, come!" This poor distracted world needs the righteousness and peace that He alone can establish. Jeremiah gives us a similarly delightful word concerning Him: "Behold, the days come, saith Jehovah, that I will raise unto David a righteous Branch, and He shall reign as King and do wisely, and shall execute judgment and justice in the earth" (Jer. 23.5-R.V.). The Gospel of Matthew presents to us our Lord as the King; and, remarkably, His first utterance recorded therein contains the word "righteousness." At Jordan, when John was disposed to refuse Him baptism, He said, "Suffer it to be so now, for thus it becometh us to fulfil all righteousness" (Matt. 3.15). Thus He would Himself practise what in the day of His power He will administer to the world. In David's great Psalm of the King, we read, "Thou lovest righteousness, and hatest wickedness" (Psalm 45.7).

In the matter of righteousness David signally failed. Joab was allowed to murder both Abner and Amasa, and pass unpunished. David's own sons Ammon and Absalom were guilty of grievous sins, and they also passed unpunished. With reference to Joab, David said, "these men the sons of Zeruiah are too hard for me," and he even said, "I am this day weak, though anointed king" (2 Sam. 3.39). Pitiful language from one who had frequently experienced the sustaining power and grace of God! But Joab was a capable military commander, and thus useful to the State! This is by no means the only occasion on which the sins of public men have been condoned. But it is not righteousness!

There is yet another explanation which covers all these sad cases. David's own sins in the matter of Uriah and Bathsheba had weakened his hands. It has been truly said that "a maimed hand cannot wield a heavy sword." Besides, had he not used Joab as his tool for the murder of Uriah? When he lay dying, he charged Solomon to deal with Joab and others whom he had spared; but the whole story is humiliating nevertheless (1 Kings 2.1-9).

Psalm 101 must here be transcribed:

A Psalm of David

1. I will sing of mercy and judgment; unto Thee, O Jehovah, will I sing.
2. I will behave myself wisely in a perfect way. O when wilt Thou come unto me? I will walk within my house with a perfect heart.
3. I will set no wicked thing before mine eyes: I hate the work of them that turn aside; it shall not cleave to me.
4. A forward heart shall depart from me: I will not know a wicked person.
5. Whoso privily slandereth his neighbour, him will I cut off: him that hath a high look and a proud heart will I not suffer.
6. Mine eyes shall be upon the faithful of the land, that they may dwell with me: he that walketh in a perfect way, he shall serve me.
7. He that worketh deceit shall not dwell within my house:

he that telleth lies shall not tarry in my sight.
8. I will early (*i.e.* every morning) destroy all the wicked of the land; that I may cut off all wicked doers from the city of Jehovah.

These were David's noble resolutions before he ascended the throne. How grievously he failed we have seen. Solomon's sentiments may be learned from the Book of Proverbs: "A king sitting on the throne of judgment scattereth away all evil with his eyes" (chap. 20.8). "Take away the wicked from before the king, and his throne shall be established in righteousness" (chap. 25.5). When Solomon had executed judgment upon Joab and others, the Holy Spirit says, "the Kingdom was established in the hand of Solomon" (1 Kings 2.46).

But in neither David nor his son do we see perfection. When penning Psalm 101 David was carried by the spirit of inspiration far beyond himself and he was led to describe the King who is yet to come. His first action will be to "send forth His angels, and they shall gather out His Kingdom all things that offend, and them which do iniquity: and shall cast them into a furnace of fire: there shall be wailing and gnashing of teeth" (Matt, 13.41-42). "The sons of Belial shall be all of them as thorns thrust away" (2 Sam 23.6). Throughout His administration every act of insubordination to the will of God will be dealt with in righteous judgment. "Righteousness shall go before Him, and shall set His footsteps on the way (J.N.D.). Truth shall spring out of the earth, and righteousness shall look down from heaven" (Psalm 85.11-13). Nothing will in that age be seen on earth that will offend the eye of God.

Psalm 101 is rather negative in its statements. We learn from it the sort of persons the King will not tolerate; Psalms 15, and 24. are more positive, and they describe those in whom the King will find pleasure, and with whom He will surround Himself in Zion. The Kingdom of God as we know it today "is not meat and drink, but righteousness and peace, and joy in the Holy

Ghost" (Rom. 14.17). May these divine excellencies characterise our lives. We stand before God in righteousness divine through the work of the Lord Jesus; let righteousness be seen in all our ways before men (1 John 3.7; Titus 3.8).

If we are not called upon in this day of grace to "cut off wicked doers from the city of the Lord," we can at least cast off from ourselves the works of darkness, and also mortify our members which are upon the earth (Rom. 13.12; Col.3.5). Thus, and thus only, shall we be righteous ones in the eyes of both God and men.

Wisdom

WHEREVER the Bible is known, Solomon is famous for his exceptional wisdom. Alas, that one so profoundly wise should have degenerated into a great fool! As the writer of the Book of Ecclesiastes, he expressed the fear that his son might be a fool (as indeed he was), but he did not appear to have been apprehensive for himself (Eccles. 2.10). Well does the Apostle say, "Let him that thinketh he standeth, take heed lest he fall" (1 Cor. 10.12).

Job in his ninth and last discourse, which occupies six chapters, speaks of the excellency of wisdom (Job 28.12-28). Having spoken of men's skill in mining and engineering (at that early date!), and their diligent search for the treasures of the earth, he exclaimed, "But where shall wisdom be found, and where is the place of understanding?" The bowels of the earth will not reveal it, and its value far exceeds that of gold and rubies. God alone can declare its true nature and value, "and unto man He said, Behold, the fear of the Lord is the *beginning* of wisdom; and the knowledge of the holy is understanding" (Prov. 9.10). Therefore until God gets His rightful place in a man's mind and heart he is incapable of viewing anything wisely. His thoughts are out of centre. His *beginning* is all wrong.

Since the days of Job and Solomon the eternal Wisdom has come into the world in the person of the Son of God. Everything must now be considered in relation to Him. "Christ is the power of God, and the wisdom of God" (1 Cor. 1.24). What can man show in the way of power in comparison with the "exceeding greatness" of the power of God "which He wrought in Christ, when He raised Him from the dead, and set Him at His own right hand in the heavenly places"? (Eph. 1.20). What wisdom can man show, with all his research, that will compare with what God revealed when He turned Calvary's disgraceful gibbet into the means of salvation and blessing for countless myriads? Men denied His beloved Son the petty dignity of kingship over the Jews, and God has given Him the headship of the universe; and all that has come to Christ, and will yet come to Him, was settled in the counsels of infinite love ages before men imbrued their hands in the blood of the Holy One! His enemies will yet be confounded at their own folly and be constrained to acknowledge the surpassing wisdom of God. "The foolishness of God is wiser than men; and the weakness of God is stronger than men" (1 Cor. 1.25). "Let no man deceive himself. If any man among you seemeth to be wise in this world. let him become a fool that he may be wise. For the wisdom of this world is foolishness with God" (1 Cor. 3.18-19). The man who leaves God and Christ out of his life's scheme is as hopelessly adrift as a vessel in a storm without chart and rudder.

Solomon was probably the most versatile monarch that has ever lived. Many of the kings who ruled England and Scotland centuries after his time could neither read or write. Their ignorance may explain their subserviency to papal delusions, to the injury of their people as well as of themselves. But no subject seemed outside the range of Solomon's knowledge. "He spoke three thousand proverbs"; good would it be for us all if we read through at least once every year those which the Holy Spirit has preserved for us. "His songs were a thousand and five"; but only one remains. Its theme is Christ, and thus it could not be allowed to lapse. It is indeed "the Song of Songs"; no other metrical composition will compare with it. The believer in Jesus, indwelt by the Holy Spirit, must be in a pitiful condition if unable to read it with sacred joy. The "song" has been the delight of the pious through the ages. What was it to Samuel Rutherford in his afflictions?

Solomon spoke also of trees, from the stately cedar of Lebanon to the humble "hyssop that springeth out of the wall." Beasts, birds, creeping things, and fishes came likewise into his discourses. He surrounded himself with all the wise men he could hear of. Several outstanding ones are named in 1 Kings 4.31, some now unknown, and some still known to us. But God's unique servant surpassed them all, - expressive type of Him with whom none in heaven or earth will compare!* "Never man spake like this Man," was said of Him even in the days of His humiliation! (John 7.46).

At this point let us listen to Solomon's own testimony. "I was my father's son, tender and only beloved in the sight of my mother. He taught me also, and said unto me, Let thine heart retain my words: keep my commandments and live. Get wisdom, get understanding; forget it not; neither decline from the words of my mouth. Forsake her not, and she shall preserve thee: love her, and she shall keep thee. Wisdom is the principal thing; therefore get wisdom; and with all thy getting get understanding. Exalt her, and she shall promote thee: she shall

---

Ethan the Ezrahite is specially named. It was he who wrote Psalm 89, a wonderful unfolding of Jehovah's loving-kindness and faithfulness with respect to the throne in Zion. The writer was carried far beyond David and Solomon to Christ. What stores of spiritual wisdom were in Ethan's heart! Yet Solomon was wiser than he!

bring thee to honour when thou dost embrace her. She shall give to thine head an ornament of grace; a crown of glory shall she deliver to thee" (Prov. 4.3-9). To this we must add the young king's comment, "Happy is the man that findeth wisdom, and the man that getteth understanding" (Prov. 3.13).

David's earnest counsel will account, at least in measure, for Solomon's answer to Jehovah in Gibeon. How remarkably He met his desire! Solomon pleaded that Israel was "so great": how could he carry the responsibility of guiding such a nation? Now compare verses 20 and 29 of 1 Kings 4., "Judah and Israel were many, as the sand which is by the sea in multitude";

"God gave Solomon wisdom and understanding exceeding much, and largeness of heart even as the sand which is on the seashore." Wisdom according to the need!

A great lesson is here! The greater the responsibility and need, the greater the divine provision to meet it. Let us take courage! Solomon's God is ours, and He may be trusted to stand by us in all the sufficiency of His wisdom and grace in any position in which He is pleased to set us, however difficult it may be. Faith can say, "I have strength for all things in Him that gives me power" (Phil. 4.13 - J.N.D.).

"In much wisdom is much grief; and he that increaseth knowledge increaseth sorrow." So we read, Solomon being the writer, in Ecclesiastes 1.18. There is truth in his words. The thinking man necessarily suffers more than the frivolous multitude. His studies give him an understanding of the evils that operate around him which others lack! Men sometimes say, "Ignorance is bliss." The man who increases his knowledge increases his capacity for suffering. But is this true where GOD is concerned? A thousand times No. The better we know our God the more we enhance our joy; and the better we understand His purposes for this poor devastated world, the more fit we are to live and testify therein.

* * * * * * * * * *

The story of the two harlots and the living babe is recorded at length as a sample of Solomon's wise administration. The suggestion to divide the babe with the sword was novel and bold, and probably without precedent in the world's history, but it brought out with such a gush the feelings of the true mother that it became perfectly clear to whom the child belonged. The king's action produced profound impression upon the people in general. "All Israel heard of the judgment which the King had judged; and they feared the King: for they saw that the Wisdom of God was in Him, to do judgment" (1 Kings 3.17-28). But the incident reminds us that perfection was not reached in Solomon's glorious reign. It is inconceivable that such a sordid case could be submitted to the arbitrament of Solomon's greater Son, God's "Holy One" (Psalm 89.19).

Supremacy and Prosperity

OUR blessed Lord once spoke with appreciation of "the lilies of the field." "Consider them," said He. "I say unto you, that Solomon in all his glory was not arrayed like one of these" (Matt. 6.28-29). From His holy heaven He had seen Solomon in his magnificent coronation robes, wrought by skilful hands; but to His mind the modest lily, work of God, presented a more attractive picture. God's saints are likened to lilies in the Song of Songs (chap. 2.2-16). May the gracious Spirit of God work in us all the lily character. No "outward adornment" will compare with it (1 Peter 3.3).

On another occasion, in view of Jewish unbelief, He said, "In this place is One greater than the temple"; and further, "a greater than Solomon is here" (Matt. 12.6, 42). The temple with its "goodly stones," and Solomon in his glory and wisdom, gave less pleasure to the heart of God than the lowly Man Who came to earth to do all His will.

But Solomon's glory, although the veriest tinsel when viewed in the light of the heavenly glory of the exalted Christ, had nevertheless a typical character and so is instructive. Never had Israel and the nations seen the like. In Solomon's day the blessing of the people reached its climax. They had-

1. The land of Jehovah's promise.
2. The city of His choice - His resting-place (Psalm 132.14).
3. The King of His appointment.
4. The Temple.

Land, City, King, Temple! Alas, that all should have been enjoyed for so short a time! Everything was soon lost by the sins of both king and people, never to be restored until the day of the Lord Jesus.

Psalm 89. may well be carefully pondered at this point. Ethan sings and speaks with rapture of Jehovah's purposes concerning His people. Both Solomon and Christ will be found in the Psalm. Solomon held the blessing of God on terms of responsibility, and thus everything was forfeited. When could God ever trust flesh? The failure of Solomon and of every other into whose hands God has entrusted great things only makes it clear that Christ is the only hope. In His day He will take up all that men have handled and lost, and He will carry through to perfection every desire and purpose of God.

Solomon's glory and power were phenomenal. "The king made a great throne of ivory, and overlaid it with pure gold. There were six steps to the throne, with a footstool of gold, which were fastened to the throne, and stays (arms) on each side of the sitting place, and two lions standing by the stays: and twelve lions stood there on the one side and on the other upon the six steps. There was not the like made in any kingdom" (2 Chron. 9.17-19). His drinking vessels were of gold - "silver was nothing accounted of in the days of Solomon." His dominion covered the whole extent of the land of promise. If it was not all occupied by Israel, it was at least brought under the authority of the king. "Solomon reigned over all kingdoms from the river unto the land of the Philistines, and unto the border of Egypt: they brought presents and served Solomon all the days of his life. . .for he had dominion over all the region on this side the river, from Tiphsah even to Azzah, over all the kings on this side the river: and he had peace on all sides round about him" (1 King 4.21-24). He not only ruled the kings, but he had their respect. "His fame was in all nations round about. . .there came of all people to hear the wisdom of Solomon, from all the kings of the earth, which had heard of his wisdom" (1 Kings 4.31-34). Faint picture of the gathering up to Jerusalem from all quarters when our Lord is there! What wonderful words He will have for them all!

Solomon's daily provision was immense, for his household was large, and his hospitality was lavish. Nehemiah's doings in Jerusalem after the break-up were humble by comparison. The latter entertained frequently "an hundred and fifty of the Jews and rulers, beside those that came unto us from the nations about." For this he required one ox and six choice sheep daily, keeping everything low because of the poverty of the returned remnant (Neh. 5.17-18). This devoted governor sought nothing for himself: only the good of the people. But Solomon required daily "ten fat oxen and twenty oxen out of the pastures, and an hundred sheep, besides harts, and roe-bucks, and fallow-deer, and fatted fowl" (1 Kings 4.22-23). Again a picture of Christ, who, when He reigns in Zion, "will abundantly bless her provision, and will satisfy her poor with bread" (Psalm 132.15). His entertainment of five thousand men, besides women and children, in the wilderness, made the people desirous of establishing Him forthwith as their king (John 6.15). But God's time was not yet.

The prosperity and tranquillity of the people was as

phenomenal as the glory and power of the king. "Judah and Israel were many, as the sand which is by the sea in multitude, eating and drinking, and making merry. . . (they) dwelt every man safely under his vine and under his fig-tree, from Dan even to Beersheba, all the days of Solomon" (1 Kings 4.20-25). Thus was fulfilled the word of Jehovah in Leviticus 26.5-6: "Your threshing shall reach unto the vintage, and the vintage shall reach unto the sowing time: and ye shall eat your bread to the full, and dwell in the land safely. And I will give peace to the land, and ye shall lie down, and none shall make you afraid." The people, as well as the king, were the head of the nations, not the tail; and they lent to many nations, but did not borrow. Said Jehovah: "All people of the earth shall see that thou art called by the name of Jehovah, and they shall be afraid of thee" (Deut. 28.10-13).

In Isaiah's day we hear the sigh of Israel's God: "Ah sinful nation, a people laden with iniquity, a seed of evil-doers, children that are corrupters: they have forsaken Jehovah, they have provoked the Holy One of Israel unto anger, they are gone away backward" (Isa. 1.4). When the Saviour approached Jerusalem for the last time, He wept over it, as He spoke of the calamities that were near at hand (Luke 19. 41-44). The foolish people threw away all that they enjoyed in the golden days of Solomon in order that they might "enjoy the pleasures of sin for a season." Well-nigh three thousand years of banishment and anguish have been their portion, and the worst has yet to come. Did space permit, we would transfer the entire Lamentations of Jeremiah to these pages; for they bring home to our hearts what a pious man, taught of the Spirit, felt concerning the disasters which have overwhelmed the erring people of Jehovah.

"If" is a small word, but tremendous issues hang upon it. All Israel's blessings were conditional upon the faithfulness of both king and people; and everything was forfeited by their evil ways, despite the earnest warnings and protests of their God. Jehovah even speaks of Himself as "rising up early, and

sending messengers to them, because He had compassion on
His people, and on His dwelling-place" (2 Chron. 36.15; Jer.
35.15. etc.). But it was of no avail. Here are a few of God's
solemn "ifs":-

To the people-
  "If thou wilt diligently hearken to the voice of Jehovah thy
    God" (Exod. 15.26).
  "If ye will obey My voice indeed, and keep My covenant"
    (Exod. 19.5).
  "If ye will fear Jehovah and serve Him" (1 Sam. 12.14).
  "If thou shalt hearken unto the voice of Jehovah thy God"
    (Deut. 28.2).

To Solomon-
  "If thou wilt walk in My ways, and keep My statues" (1
    Kings 3.14).

Now listen to the divine lament in Psalm 81.13, "Oh that My
people had hearkened unto Me, and Israel had walked in My
ways!"

But mercy is in store for Israel yet. God will never go back
upon His promises to Abraham, Isaac, and Jacob, and the
people are still "beloved for the fathers sake" (Rom. 11.28).
Woe to those who would do them harm!

The same grace which has saved both writer and reader,
once guilty sinners, will yet save guilty Israel. The people will
yet own their folly, and take the lowest possible place before
God. The law, so long gloried in although not kept, will be
surrendered as an impossible principle of blessing. Two great
sins lie at Israel's door - the violation of the law and the rejection
and murder of Christ. Psalm 1. shows us God's controversy
with the people concerning the law, and Psalm 51. His dealing
with them concerning Christ. In Isaiah's prophecy chapters
40-48 deal mainly with Israel's idolatry (in defiance of the

law), and chapters 49-57 are principally occupied with the people's rejection of Christ. Each section concludes with the solemn refrain - "there is no peace to the wicked." Israel has proved the truth of this painfully. "I will remember My covenant with thee in the days of thy youth," says Jehovah, "and I will establish unto thee an everlasting covenant. Then shalt thou remember thy ways, and be ashamed" (Ezek. 16.60-61).

Peace will return when the true Solomon sits upon "the throne of His father David." Once more they will "sit every man under his vine and under his fig-tree; and none shall make them afraid: for the mouth of Jehovah of hosts hath spoken it" (Mic. 4.4; Zech. 3.10). "The wilderness and the solitary place shall be glad for them; and the desert shall rejoice and blossom as the rose. It shall blossom abundantly, and rejoice even with joy and singing" (Isa. 35.1-2). Men shall say, "The land that was desolate is become like the garden of Eden; and the waste and desolate and ruined cities are become fenced and inhabited. Then the nations that are left round about you shall know that I Jehovah build the ruined places, and plant that which was desolate: I Jehovah hath spoken it, and I will do it" (Ezek. 36.35-36). Jewish industry apart from God seeks to antedate this, but the overwhelming Northern invasion in the day of the Antichrist will devastate the land again, but for the last time (Joel 2.1-3). The coming of the long-rejected One cannot be much longer delayed. In His hands is fulness of blessing even for the most unworthy.

The Daughter of Pharoah

IT is considered by some estimable brethren that Solomon's marriage with the daughter of Pharoah, King of Egypt, is a picture of the union of Christ and the Church - a Gentile wife sharing the throne of Jehovah with the man of His choice. This suggestion, however, presents a difficulty. When Solomon brought up the ark of Jehovah into the city of David, he felt constrained to remove his Egyptian wife elsewhere. 2 Chronicles 8.11 tells us, "Solomon brought up the daughter of Pharoah out of the city of David unto the house that he had built for her: for he said, My wife shall not dwell in the house of David King of Israel, because the places are holy, whereunto the ark of Jehovah hath come." The reason assigned for the change is startling ! Solomon felt that there was nothing in common between this Egyptian woman and the holy things of God. She was as completely out of fellowship with Solomon spiritually as Michal was with his father (although Michal was of the chosen nation - 2 Sam. 6.20). If Solomon was sensitive to the extent of removing Pharoah's daughter from proximity to the holy places, why did he marry her? "Can two walk together, except they be agreed?" (Amos 3.3). Do not his own words suggest that he had blundered in this union? 1 Kings 3.1 suggests that the affair was political in character. The sacred ordinance of marriage should never be used for such ends. True, Solomon gained the important frontier city of Gezer as dowry with his wife. The place was still held by a remnant of Canaanites, whom Egyptian forces exterminated for Solomon's benefit (1 Kings 9.16). But should not the Ephraimites have taken the place long before, trusting in God? (Josh. 16.10). The whole business was on a low level, not in keeping with Solomon's unique position as the man of God's choice. Faith is nowhere discernible in the matter, and "whatsoever is not of faith is sin" (Rom. 14.23).

It is refreshing to turn from Solomon to Christ. In Ephesians 5.25 we read that He "loved the Church, and gave Himself for it." None of those whom His grace is bringing thus nigh to Himself possessed naturally any fitness either for His holy company or for those surroundings of glory into which He will introduce His bride at the last. Solomon felt it was impossible to suit the Egyptian to the holy places of Jerusalem, her tastes being at variance with them. Christ, on the contrary, is rendering His own a continuous loving ministry in order to fit every one for all that He has in store. "He has delivered Himself up for it, that He might sanctify it, purifying it by the washing of water by the Word" (J.N.D.). The result: "that He might present the Assembly to Himself glorious, having no spot, or wrinkle or any of such things; but that it might be holy and blameless." His Bride, composed largely of Gentile sinners, will be perfectly suited to all His desire, so perfect is His work.

There was, alas, a background to Solomon's Egyptian marriage. He was in transgression even before he ascended the throne. Although very young he had already taken to wife an Ammonitish woman, and Rehoboam was the fruit of the union. Seeing that Rehoboam was forty-one years old when he began to reign, he was a babe of twelve months old when Solomon began to reign. It is twice repeated in 1 Kings 14. that "his mother's name was Naamah an Ammonitess" (vv21 & 31). The Holy Spirit mentions the fact again in 2 Chronicles 12.13. Solomon's first marriage was flagrant sin. Here is the divine command: "An Ammonite or Moabite shall not enter into the congregation of Jehovah; even to their tenth generation shall they not enter into the congregation of Jehovah for ever." (Deut. 23.3) This was thus the beginning of an evil course which led ultimately to Solomon's ruin, and also to the ruin of the whole order of things of which he was the divinely appointed centre. First, a woman from Ammon; then a woman from Egypt; and later a whole host of women from near and far, who brought their abominable idolatries into Jehovah's land, and into Solomon's heart. The Egyptian princess is again expressly mentioned in 1 Kings 11.1 as if she were the advance guard of this host of evil. "King Solomon loved many strange (or foreign) women, together with the daughter of Pharoah."

Brethren, let us watch against the beginning of fleshey indulgence in any form. In the light of the great truth that in God's account we have "died with Christ," let us "mortify our members which are upon the earth; fornication, uncleanness, inordinate affection, evil concupiscence, and covetousness which is idolatry" (Col. 3.5). If fornication is no special snare to us, its twin-brother covetousness may be. Let us beware. It has been truly said: "The slippery path of sin is always trodden with accelerated steps, because the first sin tends to weaken in the soul the authority and power of that which alone can prevent our committing still greater sins - that is, the Word of God, as well as the consciousness of His presence, which imparts to the Word all its practical power over us."

"Be not unequally yoked together with unbelievers: for what fellowship hath righteousness with unrighteousness? And what communion hath light with darkness? And what concord hath Christ with Belial? Or what part hath he that believeth with an unbeliever?" (2 Cor. 6.14-15).

"Be ye holy, for I am holy" (1 Peter 1.16).

Provision for the House

WHEN the people of God are in a healthy spiritual condition, the funds are healthy also and the Treasurers have no anxiety. The spiritual affections being in full flow, all that is required for the maintenance of the Lord's work is in full flow also. When Jehovah asked Israel in the wilderness to prepare Him a habitation, the offerings were so abundant that the people had to be restrained. Bezaleel and his helpers reported to Moses, "The people bring much more than enough for the service of the work, which Jehovah commanded to make" (Exod. 36.5). Their hard-earned Egyptian wages, secured for them by Jehovah Himself before they left that land (Exod. 3.22), were willingly laid at the feet of their Saviour-God. Even so, their devotedness will not compare with that of the poor widow upon whom the eye of the Lord Jesus rested in the days of His flesh (Luke 21.2-4).

There was a pitiful contrast in Malachi's day. The remnant returned from Babylon, to whom God had shown much favour, became so cold and indifferent in their religious exercises that even the prescribed tithes and offerings were not brought in (Mal. 3.8-10). Voluntary offerings - the "extras" which manifest the love of the heart, were absolutely non-existent.

When Hezekiah appealed to the people concerning the needs of the house of Jehovah, he was delighted with the result. "When Hezekiah and the princes came and saw the heaps, they blessed Jehovah and His people Israel" (2 Chron. 31.8). The pious king's feelings were similar to those of Paul in Philippians 4.17 - "Not that I desire a gift: but I desire fruit that may abound to your account."

The coming of the Holy Spirit at Pentecost produced a marvellous wave of surrender amongst the newly saved. Their joy was great. Behold how they stood with God! Having been convicted of the awful crime of killing the Son of God, they had come to understand that His death was part of a divine counsel of grace, and that in virtue of His death and resurrection they were forgiven and blessed. Their affections followed earth's rejected One to the place where He had gone, and this made the things of earth of but small value in their eyes. Accordingly, they "sold their possessions and goods, and parted them to all men, as every man had need" (Acts 2.45). They did not understand *union*, for the Mystery had not yet been revealed, but they practised *unity* most blessedly. There were no suffering poor in the early Church in Jerusalem. Barnabas is specially named in connection with this remarkable wave of surrender. "Having land, he sold it, and brought the money, and laid it at the Apostles' feet" (Acts 4.37). This community of goods was not demanded of them; but the voluntariness of it made it very precious in the sight of Him who for our sakes became poor that we through His poverty might be rich (2 Cor. 8.9).

A community of goods was only practicable while the Church was limited to one city. As the truth spread, and Assemblies sprung up elsewhere, a different condition of things obtained. Some were rich, and others were poor. The Corinthians were wealthy, but the Assemblies of Macedonia were poor (2 Cor. 8.1-2). When need arose in one quarter, it was met from another, for the Church of God is one throughout the earth. The first example of this is recorded in Acts 11.27-30. A general famine was predicted by Agabus, and the brethren in Antioch, "every man according to his ability, determined to send relief unto the brethren which dwelt in Judea." The threatened trouble was to be " a great dearth throughout the world." Thus Antioch was in danger, as well as Judea, yet they sent their gifts! Unselfish love, assuredly! This is a greater and more enduring bond than ecclesiastical regulations, however well intentioned they may be. Judea might well have replied to Antioch, "the things which were sent from you are an odour of a sweet smell, a sacrifice acceptable, well-pleasing to God" (Phil. 4.18).

Coming now to the Temple, Solomon was the man chosen by God to build it. "Solomon thy son, he shall build My house and My courts, for I have chosen him to be My son, and I will be his father" (1 Chron. 28.6). But the plans were nevertheless given to David. "All this," said David, "Jehovah made me understand in writing by His hand upon me, even all the works of this pattern" (1 Chron. 28.19). These plans David entrusted to Solomon, "the pattern of the porch, and of the houses thereof," etc (1 Chron. 28.11). David stood upon higher ground in relation to Jehovah than his distinguished son. He was as truly a vessel of divine inspiration as Moses in the wilderness. What honour will compare with conscious nearness to God?

In all his afflictions David delighted in the thought of a house for God. The humble tabernacle was very dear to him meantime. "Jehovah, I have loved the habitation of Thy house, and the place where Thy glory dwelleth" (Psalm 26.8). When his wanderings ceased, and he dwelt in peace in "a house of cedar," it did not please David that the ark of God still abode in curtains (2 Sam. 7.2). The intensity of his desire is expressed in Psalm 132. But however godly his desire, and however acceptable to God, the man of peace, not the man of war, must be the builder of God's house (1 Chron. 22.8-9). Psalm 132 looks far beyond the day of Solomon to Christ's millennial reign. Then a Temple will be reared that will excel in glory anything that earth has yet seen. Ezekiel's last nine chapters describe with much detail the new conditions.

But if David must not build the house for God, he could at least make preparation for it, and this he did with all his heart. Hear him: "I have prepared with all my might for the house of my God.... I have set my affection to the house of my God" (1 Chron. 29.2-3). This is what God loves to see in His people. Yet the day came when He had to say to Israel, "Who is there among you that would even shut the doors for nought?" (Mal. 1.10). "Behold, what a weariness is it!" (Mal. 1.13) said their poor wayward hearts. All their sorrows have come upon them because they "served not Jehovah their God with joyfulness, and with gladness of heart, for the abundance of all things" (Deut. 28.47). When David brought the ark up to Zion, he "danced before Jehovah with all his might" (2 Sam. 6.14). The same holy enthusiasm manifested itself in him in old age and imparted itself to Solomon, the princes, and the people generally. The whole of the two concluding chapters of 1 Chronicles should be read, for they describe the unity of mind and heart amongst all classes in Israel concerning the great project of building a house for Jehovah.

David's attitude towards the people while encouraging them to build for God is very beautiful. "Hear me, my brethren" (1 Chron. 28.2). Jehovah desired Israel's king, when the time came that they would have one, to read the book of the law daily "that his heart be not lifted up above *his brethren*" (Deut. 17.20). There is nothing of the Oriental despot in this. God's king must not tyrannise over, but "feed Jacob His people and Israel His inheritance" (Psalm 78.71). The great King of Kings, when He sits upon the throne of His glory with angels in attendance will acknowledge lowly men who have preached His word as "My brethren" (Matt. 25 40).

The offerings for the work of the Temple were immense. David had stored up vast sums, partly the spoil of his conquests; from his own fortune he gave largely; and the princes and people added their quota. The figures stand thus:-

From the Treasury,	100,000	talents of	gold.
(1 Chron. 22.14)	1,000,000	"	silver.
From the King,	3,000	"	gold.
(1 Chron. 29. 4)	7,000	"	silver.
From the Princes, etc.,	5,000	"	gold.
(1 Chron. 29.7)	10,000	"	silver.

Reckoning the gold at £5,475 per talent of 114lbs. weight, and the silver at £342 per talent, the total amounts to £591,300,000 gold and £347,814,000 silver. This is the value of the precious metals. The brass, iron, and precious stones would swell the amount further.

"The people rejoiced, for that they offered willingly, because with perfect heart they offered willingly to Jehovah, and David the king also rejoiced with great joy." The king in his public thanksgiving took no credit for this lavishness, saying, "Who am I, and what is my people, that we should be able to offer so willingly after this sort? for all things come of Thee, and of

Thine own have we given Thee" (Chron. 29.9, 14).

He then called upon the people to bless Jehovah. "And all the congregation blessed Jehovah God of their fathers, and bowed down their heads and worshipped Jehovah and the king." Burnt-offerings followed on a large scale, and the people "did eat and drink before Jehovah on that day with great gladness" (1 Chron. 29.20-22). Why? Because their faithful God had consented to dwell in their midst, and had allowed them the honour of building the house for His name.

Thus everything was prepared before David's death for the first of the five Temples which are connected with Jerusalem in the sacred records.

(1) Solomon's Temple, now to be constructed.

(2) Zerubbabel's Temple, erected by the pious remnant after the return from Babylon (Ezra 1.3).

(3) Herod's Temple, built by Jews in his day, and desecrated by him (Rev. 11.1; 2 Thess.2. 4; Matt. 24.15).

(5) The Millennial Temple, specifications given in Ezekiel 40., etc.

When the Lord Jesus died, the veil of the Temple was rent in the midst, God thus signifying that the old order was abolished. The time has now come when neither in Jerusalem nor in Samaria's mountain should men worship the Father (John iv. 21-24).

* * * * * * * * * *

A few words may well be added here concerning worship in "the hour that now is" (*i.e.* Christianity). Its fullest expression is found in John 4.21-24. Those who suggest that the Samaritan woman raised the question of places of worship in order to turn aside the keen edge of the Lord's exposure of her evil life are not quite just. What she had in her mind more probably was the difficulty as to where He could be found of whose holiness the

Speaker was making her conscious. The Samaritans said one thing and the Jews another; where then was the true religious centre? The Lord replied, "Woman, *believe Me*" - note His words! He speaks with authority; He knows God as no other could know Him; and He only can reveal His thoughts. "Believe Me, the hour cometh when ye shall neither in this mountain, nor yet at Jerusalem, worship the Father." Samaritan worship never had a divine standing - it was an abominable conglomeration from the beginning (2 Kings 17.41); Judaism, on the contrary, was originally of God. But both must stand aside now. *The Father* stands revealed in the person of the Son of His love; all distance is ended. Sanctuaries and ecclesiastics are worse than useless now. The place of assembly matters little - school-house, barn, private dwelling, etc. The Father seeks those who are conscious of intimate relationship with Himself, and who will worship Him in spirit and in truth. Nothing else will satisfy Him "in the hour that now is." It was doubtless a delight to Him when Hezekiah reopened and repaired the slighted Temple (2 Chron. 29.3); but such service could have no value today.

In verse 22 the Lord said, "the hour *cometh*," for God had not yet definitely rejected the earthly sanctuary. Ere long the veil would be divinely rent, but the action was still future. In verse 23 the Lord goes further, saying, "the hour cometh *and now is*." The subject here is not the place of worship, but the character of it. The Son having come, He who is now revealed by the sweet name Father, requires something more than forms, however scripturally correct. "The hour cometh, and now is, when the true worshippers shall worship the Father in spirit and in truth: for the Father seeketh such to worship Him." Precious thought! the Son was on earth seeking sinners; and the Father by His revelations in and through the Son was seeking worshippers. Thus, even before the Temple was divinely disowned, there was more for God in the adoration of Mary of Bethany than in all the gorgeous ritual of the Aaronic priesthood

(John 12.3).

"In spirit and in truth" does not mean merely that all worship must be in the power of the Holy Spirit, and in accordance with revealed truth (although that is deeply important); it means also a spiritual and truthful condition. Hence the Lord's words in verse 24: "God is a spirit: and they that worship Him must worship Him in spirit and in truth." Not now the "Father," but "God." Being what He is, He insists that those who approach Him should do so in this way and condition. *"Must."* Neither Peter nor Barnabas were in a spiritual and truthful condition when they dissimulated at Antioch; Paul, who was, faithfully exposed and rebuked their dishonesty (Gal. 2.11-14).

National worship, expressed in ritual, was once according to God, at least as far as Israel was concerned, and it will be so again in the millennial age, as Ezekiel's concluding chapters tell us; but both in the past and in the future for such worship a visible sanctuary and a priesthood are necessary. All this is entirely out of place in the hour that now is.

The gathering centre now is not a building, but a name. "Where two or three are gathered together unto My name there am I in the midst of them" (Matt. 18.20). This supposes grateful souls attracted by what they have found in the Name of their Lord coming together to speak to God and to one another about Him. This is heart-exercise, very precious to the Father and the Son, and very delightful to the worshippers themselves.

The Temple

THE Tabernacle and the Temple differ considerably in the matter of interpretation. It has pleased the Spirit of God to give us the New Testament Epistle to the Hebrews as His inspired commentary on the institutions of the former, but no New Testament book opens up for us the latter. This is the more remarkable because the Tabernacle had long passed away, and the Temple was functioning in Jerusalem. The explanation is that the position of the saints when the Hebrews were addressed answered more to Tabernacle than to Temple conditions. For the world had become a wilderness to them because of their identification with the rejected Christ. Nevertheless, as we meditate upon the temple and its vessels as described in the books of the Kings and Chronicles, spiritual suggestions will not be lacking.

There is nothing superfluous in the Scriptures, although we are not always able to grasp the significance of its varied contents. The question may easily arise in some minds, Why have we double accounts of the reigns of David, Solomon, and other kings? Why the Books of the Chronicles seeing that there were already existent the Books of the Kings? Examination will show that the Holy Spirit had His special aim and purpose in connection with each set of books. It is observable, for example, that in the Chronicles the sins of David and Solomon are omitted, while their triumphs and glories are emphasized. Also, as we look through the divine instructions concerning the Temple, we shall find some striking variations between the two accounts. As a general statement, it may be affirmed that the teaching of the Books of the Kings is moral, and the teaching of the Chronicles is typical. In the later books David and Solomon are foreshadows of Christ, but in the earlier books we see the men as they really were in their weakness and failure. It seems suitable that the typical should be prominent in the Chronicles, for the books were written after the return from Babylon, when the Holy Spirit sought to cheer the faith of the pious remnant with the glories of the coming Christ by the ministry of Haggai, Zechariah, and others (Ezra 5.1).

The Threshing-Floor Site

What was it that constrained David to say when standing upon the threshing-floor of Ornan the Jubusite, "This is the house of the Lord God, and this is the altar of the burnt-offering for Israel?" (1 Chron. 22.1). There was no direct word from God to this effect. David was a man of spiritual perception, and the pardoning grace of God expressed at that spot suggested to his heart that in that place Israel's Jehovah would delight to dwell. The grievous sin of numbering the people (mainly that the king might know how many soldiers he had!) brought down judgment. David's humble repentance, and his pleading for the suffering sheep, brought him an angel from Jehovah bidding him set up an altar in Ornan's threshing-floor. As the smoke of the sacrifice ascended to heaven, Jehovah answered by fire, and He commanded the destroying angel to sheathe his sword (1 Chron. 21.). This intervention of God in grace suggested to David that Jehovah had thus indicated His choice of site for the sanctuary. Accordingly, when building-time came, we read, "Solomon began to build the house of Jehovah at Jerusalem in Mount Moriah, where He appeared unto David his father, in the place that David had prepared in the threshing-floor of Ornan the Jebusite" (2 Chron. 3.1).

God delights to dwell with men, but it is only possible on the ground of accomplished redemption. In Patriarchal times He visited His own and communed with them, but He sought no dwelling-place with them. But when He took Israel into relationship with Himself on the ground of the blood of the lamb, He said, "Let them make Me a sanctuary, that I may dwell among them" (Exod. 25.8). When the victorious Christ went up on high having finished His great redemption work on earth, the Holy Spirit came down to build for God a habitation amongst the saints (Eph. 2.22). In keeping with this great divine principle, Solomon was to build the Temple of Jehovah on the spot where the sacrifice was offered and accepted. It was in the same neighbourhood that Abraham laid Isaac upon the altar (Gen. 22.2).

We note also that the Temple was to be built upon the threshing floor of a Gentile. Hiram, King of Tyre, another Gentile, collaborated heartily with both David and Solomon in the great work (1 Kings 5). Thus Israel's God had Gentiles before His mind to share the blessedness of His presence on earth amongst His people. "Mine house shall be called a house of prayer for all the peoples" (Isa. 56.7). Just a hint in advance of the largeness and universality of God's grace in this Gospel day.

Kings and Chronicles

It is not in vain that the Holy Spirit has given us four presentations of Christ in the New Testament. Each Evangelist, as surely we all know, had his own line given him by God; and in result we have all that the all-wise Spirit judged our limited capacity could receive concerning the wondrous theme (John 21.25). In like manner the Books of Kings and Chronicles give us two views of the Temple. In Kings it is looked at as the dwelling-place of God, with special reference to the Millennial Kingdom; in Chronicles the Temple is rather the seat of divine government, and the place of approach for God's people. This will account for the omission of the Brazen Altar and the Veil in Kings, both being reserved for the Chronicles. The chambers that were built into the walls of the house round about are a special feature of the Kings account. They were designed for the occupation of those who served in the sanctuary, for God delights to have men dwelling with Him. The attitude of the large Cherubim in the Holy of Holies, looking down the house as if they would fain look outside, is noted in Chronicles alone. This suggests that when the Kingdom of David's greater Son is established righteousness will look abroad no longer in judgment, but in blessing upon men. Other points of difference between the two descriptions of the Temple will be noticed by the careful reader. Nothing in God's blessed Word is without significance.

Jachin and Boaz

The Holy Spirit in 1 Kings 6.1 dates the building of the Temple from Israel's deliverance from Egypt. Thus would He emphasize the fact that it was amongst a people saved by sovereign grace Jehovah was about to make His abode. The work was commenced in the fourth year of Solomon's reign "in the month Zif, which is the second month." This month corresponds with the British May. Zif means "splendour". Spring was in its glory, physically and otherwise. Israel was about to experience a glorious summer-time of blessing and prosperity. Alas, that it did not continue. The unfaithful nation has passed through a long dark night of sorrow since. But summer is approaching, for "HE is nigh, even at the doors" (Matt. 24.33).

The Temple was 60 cubits long, 20 cubits broad, and 30 cubits high. In its breadth and length it was double the size of the Tabernacle. The Holy of Holies was 20 cubits long, and the Holy place 40 cubits. In the front of the house broadways was a porch 20 cubits long and 10 cubits broad (1 Kings 6.3). The great pillars are described with much detail in 1 Kings 7. 15-22; much more briefly in 2 Chronicles 3.15-17. They were named Jachin meaning "He will establish," and Boaz, "In Him is strength." These great pillars, each about 18 cubits high, were a public testimony that stability is found in Christ, and only in Christ. Early in the building operations, Jehovah spoke afresh to Solomon. "Concerning this house which thou art in building, if thou wilt walk in My statues, and execute My judgments, and keep all My commandments to walk in them: then will I perform My word as to thee, which I spake unto David thy father: and I will dwell among the children of Israel, and will not forsake My people Israel" (1 Kings 6.11-13). Here again is the fatal "if". Everything at the moment depended upon the faithfulness of king and people. All was soon lost, never to be restored until the day of the Lord Jesus. But "the gifts and calling of God are without repentance" (Rom. 11.29), and He will yet fulfil all His promises of grace to Abraham, Isaac, and Jacob. Such is the evil and instability of poor flesh, that each one of us must humbly say, "Saved by grace alone; this is all my plea."

The brass (more probably "copper" or "bronze") of which the pillars were made was brought from Syria by David in war, so we are told in 1 Chronicles 18.8. Brass signifies the righteousness of God in judgment. Hence its use in the Altar of Burnt-offerings. Four figures of righteousness are found in Scripture:-

Gold - Intrinsic divine righteousness.
Brass (or copper) - Divine righteousness as applied to man in judgment.
Linen - "The righteousness of the saints" (Rev. 19.8).
Filthy Rags - The righteousness of the flesh (Isa. 64.6).

The ornamentations of the pillars suggest what Christ works for and in His own. "*Nets* of checker work": He has caught us out of the sea of humanity for Himself (Matt. 13.47; Luke 5.10). "Wreaths of *chain* work": He binds and secures all whom He acquires (Hosea 11.4). "*Pomegranates*"are frequently used in Scripture as emblems of fruitfulness. All who are Christ's are meant to be fruitful. "Upon the top of the pillars was *lily* work": the lily character, purity and lowliness, is precious in His sight. Solomon's massive brazen pillars were in the Lord's thoughts in His promise to the overcomer in Philadelphia: "I will make him a pillar in the temple of My God and He shall go no more out." What encouragement to all who with little strength seek to keep His word and not deny His name! Looked down upon to-day by the great ones of ecclesiastical Christendom; small here and now; but made great and notable in the day of recompense by our appreciative Lord. Where will others be then?

"He will establish: in Him is strength" - precious assurance both for Israel and for ourselves. He is willing: He is able. David's royal house has forfeited everything by unfaithfulness; but Christ will restore it all in the day of His power. Meantime, Solomon's noble pillars have been broken up as "scrap," and carried to Babylon (Jer. 27.19-22; 52.17-23). The Holy Spirit dwells mournfully upon their beauty whilst recording their destruction.

The Chambers

"Against the wall of the house he built chambers round about... both of the temple and of the oracle" (1 Kings 6.5). The Tabernacle had nothing answering to this; but the Temple in contrast with the Tabernacle represents a settled condition of things, for wars were at an end, and rest had come. Privileged indeed were the men who were thus permitted to dwell with God. We are reminded of the longing of David's heart as expressed in Psalm 27.4: "One thing have I desired of Jehovah, that will I seek after, that I may dwell in the house of Jehovah all the days of my life, to behold the beauty of Jehovah, and to enquire in His Temple." He spoke also of the joy of it. "Blessed is the man whom Thou choosest, and causest to approach unto Thee, that he may dwell in Thy courts: we shall be satisfied with the goodness of Thy house, even of Thy holy temple" (Psalm 65.4). The natural man understands nothing of this. The thought of God is repulsive to him. Gladly would he flee to the uttermost parts of the universe if thereby he could get away from God. Every atom of longing after God; yea, of delight in God that we discover within ourselves is the fruit of sovereign grace. The Apostle strikes a high note in Romans 5.11: "We joy in God through our Lord Jesus Christ, by whom we have received the reconciliation."

The Lord Jesus had the Temple-chambers in mind when He said, "In My Father's house are many mansions (abodes)." In John 2.16 He called the Jewish Temple "My father's house," and in chapter 14.2 He applies the same title to Heaven. At His coming we shall find ourselves in the presence of God known to us as Father; we shall be in the company of the Son; we shall bear His image; and we shall share with Him the infinite wealth of the Father's love.

The Temple-chambers were built in three stories, the higher being reached by winding stairs. The lowest stories were five cubits broad, the middle were six cubits, and the third were seven cubits. Is this meant to suggest continual progress in the Father's house above?

There is a beautiful notice of the chambers in 1 Chronicles 9.33 (Revised Version): "These are the singers, heads of fathers' houses of the Levites, who dwelt in the chambers and were free from other service: for they were employed in their work day and night." Delightful picture! Elderly men, living with Israel's God in His house, and released from all other service but praise! The time may come when some of us may have to cease active labour, but we can still praise our God. If our hearts are in tune!

In the midst of the instructions concerning the chambers in 1 Kings 6. we find these remarkable words : "the house when it was in building, was built of stone made ready before it was brought thither: so that there was neither hammer nor axe nor any tool of iron heard in the house while it was in building." A colossal work wrought without noise! How unlike man's methods! God is preparing a building for Himself to-day. It is composed of living materials - sinners saved by grace. "The whole building fitly framed together groweth unto a holy temple in the Lord" (Eph. 2.21). In the midst of all the clamour and turmoil of earth this work of God is proceeding. Unostentatiously, but surely, the work grows, and it will be seen in glorious result at the Lord's return. Unlike Solomon's Temple, it will never be overthrown.

The Walls

If the Church is to be God's holy Temple eternally, the walls of

Solomon's Temple will show us something pictorially of our future state. The stones for the walls were fully prepared away from Jerusalem. God is to-day getting His stones out of nature's quarry by means of the Gospel. Evangelists are God's quarry men, and pastors and teachers are His masons, by their unfoldings of Christ shaping and fashioning the stones according to the mind of God. Direct divine dealing in the way of suffering also helps largely towards the desired end. David's afflictions moulded his character as uninterrupted prosperity could never have done. But no stone was seen in Solomon's Temple (1 Kings 6.18). All were completely covered with refined silver (1 Chron. 29.4). In like manner, all that we were by nature is covered by Christ's redemption. The walls were also covered with boards of cedar. In the Tabernacle shittim wood is prominent. It was the incorruptible acacia of the desert, the only wood that was available there. In the Temple the principal woods used were the cedar and the olive. The shittim wood suggests what was true of our blessed Lord even when in wilderness circumstances; the cedar points to what will be true of the saints in glory. "This corruptible must put on incorruption, and this mortal must put on immortality" (1 Cor. 15.53).

The cedar-wood boards were beautifully carved. Cherubim, palm-trees, and open flowers were wrought upon them, and all were covered with gold. The walls were treated exactly as the doors, which will come before us in due course. Seeing that the doors typify Christ, who is the only way to God, the carved doors remind us that we shall be like Christ when the work of grace is completed in glory. "The whole house (Solomon) overlaid with gold" (1 Kings 6.22). "All was bright with the glory of divine righteousness that distinguished the throne of God which was placed there" (J.N.D.). Gold being the most precious of metals is frequently used in Scripture as symbolical of that which is of God.

Even the floor-boards were covered with gold. For the Tabernacle no floor was provided; the feet of the priests trod the desert sand. In the Holy City Jerusalem "the street is pure gold, as it were transparent glass" (Rev. 21.21). What a spectacle of glory and majesty was the interior of Solomon's Temple! Above, the ceiling was "overlaid with fine gold" (2 Chron. 3.5); below, the priests walked upon gold-"gold of Parvain," says the record, as if to suggest to us that only the best was used. All around the ministering priests gold glittered; and as if this were not glorious enough, even the gold was "garnished with precious stones for beauty" (2 Chron. 3.6). Truly, when we look around us in "God's eternal day," not at a mere material structure, but at the glorified saints who will form His holy temple, our eyes will behold everything that is expressive of Christ. None of His divine graces will be lacking in a single saint. "What hath God wrought!" (Num. 23.23).

The Great Cherubim

One of the most unique features of Solomon's Temple were the great cherubim which were set up in the Oracle, or Holy of Holies. They were in addition to the gold figures which were upon the ark. The ark was exactly the same in the Temple as in the Tabernacle, save as regards its contents. The large cherubim were each ten cubit high (about fifteen feet); and each had two wings. "Five cubits was the one wing of the cherub, and five cubits the other wing of the cherub: from the uttermost part of the one wing unto the uttermost part of the other were ten cubits" (1 Kings 6.24). Thus the breadth of the wings was as the height of the cherubim themselves. They touched the walls of the Oracle on either side, and they touched each other in the middle. They were made of olive wood, and were covered with gold. (The four wings are put together in 2 Chronicles 3.11 - "twenty cubits long").

The cherubim have been well described as "God's judical executive, to whomsoever entrusted, and in whatsoever circumstances displayed." They do not appear to be a distinct order in the creation of God; they are rather symbolical figures.

In His ways of government and judgment God sometimes uses angels and sometimes men. Whichever it may be, the instruments employed would be God's cherubim for the moment.

Their faces (given not in 1 Kings, but in Ezekiel 1.) suggest to us the varied qualities of God's dealings in government and in judgment. The *man's* face suggests intelligence; the *lion's* face power; the *eagle's* face rapidity of execution; and the face of the *ox* suggests patience.

The cherubim are mentioned for the fourth time in Scripture in connection with the Temple. (1) In Genesis 3.24 we see them placed forbiddingly at the gate of the garden after Adam's sin (living creatures doubtless). (2) In Exodus 25.18-20 we see golden cherubim upon the ark, beaten out of the same sheet of gold as the mercy-seat. The contrast between these Scripture passages is instructive. The executors of God's judgment who are seen opposed to transgressors in Genesis 3. are seen in Exodus 25. looking down peacefully upon the mercy-seat from which the blood of the sacrifice was never lacking. Blessed be God, the atoning blood of Christ makes blessing sure for sinful men, and puts judgment far away. (3) The cherubic symbol comes before us next (but in the singular) in 2 Samuel 22.11: "He rode upon a cherub, and did fly: and He was seen upon the wings of the wind." This is really part of Psalm 18., a rapturous song written by David "in the day that Jehovah had delivered him out of the hand of all his enemies, and out of the hand of Saul." It is a remarkable outpouring. David was carried by the Spirit far beyond the circumstances of his own case. Israel's deliverance from Egypt is also in the Psalm; and, what is much more important, the Psalm speaks of the deliverance of Christ from the power of death, and from all other foes. He becomes "head of the nations." The cherub is introduced into the Psalm as expressive of the righteous government of God acting on behalf of the objects of His favour.

In 2 Chronicles 3.13 we have the interesting statement that the Temple cherubim "stood on their feet, and their faces were inward." The margin reads "toward the house." Now, seeing that the cherubim were situated at the far end of the Temple, "towards the house" would in result mean "outwards," for they were looking in the direction of the front door. There we have the delightful suggestion, so fully taught in the prophetic word, that in the day of Kingdom-glory all that God is in righteous government will look abroad in blessing upon men - not Israel only,but all nations. Judgment will have done its needful work.

The Doors

The doors and the walls were alike in their beauty, and together they speak of Christ, and of what divine grace will work in those who are His. The pitiful lament of Psalm 74. comes to mind here. Asaph describes the desolation of the sanctuary by an outside foe. In measure this Psalm was fulfilled in the days of Nebuchadnezzar; but its complete fulfilment awaits the period of the "great tribulation." The King of the North will come down with overwhelming hosts; and because of the evil of the Jewish mass, he will be allowed to wreck his vengeance on their land and sanctuary (Dan. 11.40; Joel 2.). The pious remnant will feel the position keenly. "A man was famous according as he had lifted up his axe upon a thicket of trees. But now they break down the carved work thereof with axes and hammers" (Psalm 74.5-6). Men once famous for felling trees now spending their strength in destroying the sanctuary of God! Heart-breaking to those who loved the house for the sake of the One who dwelt therein. Asaph was a contemporary of David. It is not certain that he lived to see the Temple built, yet he writes thus graphically of its destruction! The spirit of prophecy is divinely wonderful. By its means God "calleth the things which be not as though they were" (Rom. 4.17).

But 1 King 6. speaks of palmy days when the blessing of Jehovah rested upon Israel, before the sin and folly of both king and people blasted everything. The recorder appears to speak

of two sets of doors: in verse 31-32 folding doors into the
Oracle, thus separating the holy place from the holiest of all;
and in verses 32-35 folding doors into the Temple itself, the
entrance into the Oracle being slightly the narrower of the two
sets. The Oracle doors were made from the olive tree and the
Temple doors from the fir tree. The Revisers in their margin,
and J.N. Darby in his text, think the cypress to be meant rather
than the fir. The following Scriptures connect this tree with
desirability and beauty - Isaiah 55.13; 60.13; Hosea 14.8. A
suitable type of Christ, assuredly! The doors were carved with
cherubim, for this blessed One will rule and execute judgment
for God; with palm-trees, for victory is with Him; and with
"half-open flowers" (J.N.D.), suggestive that there are with
Him always greater and more delightful things to come. Over
all this was placed gold, typical of the righteousness and glory
of God. Even the hinges of the doors were gold (1 Kings 7.50).
The lintel and side posts of both sets of doors were made of
olive-wood. The power of the Spirit is in mind in this. Only by
His power are we able to avail ourselves of Christ for access
into the divine presence. Ephesians 2.18 gives us a sweet
statement in few words of our great privilege as men saved by
grace. "Through Him (Christ) we have access by one Spirit
unto the Father."

The Molten Sea

This great receptacle for water was placed in the outer court
of the Temple. Its full capacity was 3000 baths (about 22,000
gallons); the usual quantity therein was 2000 baths. In
2 Chronicles 4. the molten sea follows the brazen altar, with
which in its teaching it was morally connected, but in
1 Kings 7. it follows the pillars Jachin and Boaz, the brazen altar
being omitted altogether.

The molten sea took the place of the laver in the Tabernacle,
but there are interesting points of difference between the two
vessels. The laver was made from the women's mirrors

(Exod. 38.8); the sea was made from the spoils of David's conquests (1 Chron. 18.8). The mirrors suggest renunciation on the part of those who gave them; the spoils speak of victory, in keeping with the Kingdom glories which are set forth in the reign of Solomon. The size and capacity of the laver is not stated; for the sea these particulars are recorded. Both laver and molten sea were for the use of the priests. From these vessels they drew water for the cleansing of their hands and feet when serving in the sanctuary of God. When Israel's priests were consecrated, they underwent a total washing (Exod. 29.4). In Hebrews 10.22 and John 13.10 this is alluded to as typical of what we have experienced spiritually. The New Birth is meant. But more than this is required in those who would draw near to a holy God. The New Birth has made us in nature meet for His presence; but the laver and the molten sea teach us that we must also be meet in practice if we would enjoy His presence. The Psalmist said when confessing his love for Jehovah's house, "I will wash my hands in innocency; so will I compass Thine altar, O Jehovah" (Psalm 26.6). Grace has made a "holy priesthood" of the whole household of faith, but holiness demands purity of thought and life in us all. The Book of Leviticus was the guide-book of the Aaronic priests, and throughout purity is inculcated. Chapter 10. is particularly solemn in its instructions and warnings, having been occasioned by the impiety of Nadab and Abihu. God resents irreverence and carelessness in the holy things, as the Corinthians experienced painfully (1 Cor. 11.30).

The molten sea, unlike the laver, "stood upon twelve oxen, three looking toward the north, and three looking toward the west, and three looking toward the south, and three looking toward the east: and the sea was set above them, and all their hinder parts were inward" (1 Kings 7.25; 2 Chron. 4. 4). In all probability there were pipes running downward through the mouths of the oxen whereby the water, when needed, flowed forth. Possibly the Lord had this in view when He stood and cried on the great day of the feast of tabernacles, "If any man thirst let him come unto Me and drink. He that believeth on me, as the scripture hath said, out of his belly shall flow rivers of living water" (John 7.37-38). In the great kingdom age the water of the Word will first be applied to Israel. "In that day there shall be a fountain opened to the house of David, and to the inhabitants of Jerusalem for sin and for uncleanness" (Zech. 13.1). "Then will I sprinkle clean water upon you, and ye shall be clean: from all your filthiness, and from all your idols will I cleanse you" (Ezek. 36.25). The pious remnant, preserved through the great tribulation, nucleus of the new nation, will not then need to teach every man his neighbour and every man his brother, "Know Jehovah," for all will know Him, and that as a pardoning God (Jer. 31.34). Great spiritual activity will result. "Out of Zion shall go forth the law, and the Word of Jehovah from Jerusalem" (Isa. 2.3). "They shall declare My glory among the Gentiles" (Isa. 66.19). "The remnant of Jacob shall be among the Gentiles as a dew from Jehovah, as showers upon the grass" (Micah 5.7). The ox is in Scripture a type of the patient labourer for God: twelve is the number of Israel's tribes. Under the mighty impulse of the latter-day outpouring of the Holy Spirit, Israel will be filled with desire that all the nations should know their God, and join with them in songs of joy (Psalm 67). Blessed contrast to their attitude during this day of grace. Their determined hostility, and their evil efforts to hinder the Gospel being preached to the Gentiles is described in 1 Thessalonians 2.16; Acts 13.45; 14.2-19. But when the Redeemer comes to Zion, and their hearts are wrought upon by divine grace, they will realise the purpose of God in their election, and will gladly throw themselves into the current of the Spirit's operations, thus spreading blessing far and wide. Did not God say to Abraham, "in thy seed shall all the nations of the earth be blessed?" (Gen. 22.18). For Israel's conversion the world's blessing waits.

Israel will in that day, as compared with other nations, stand in priestly nearness to God. At Sinai He said, "If you will obey

My voice... ye shall be unto Me a kingdom of priests" (Exod. 19.6). This has never yet been realised. In Hosea 4.6 we hear the voice of Israel's indignant God, "I will reject thee, that thou shalt be no priest to Me." But in the day of kingdom-glory, "ye shall be named the priests of Jehovah: men shall call you the ministers of our God" (Isa. 61.6). The knowledge of God and His great salvation will be spread universally. The twelve oxen under the molten sea looked north, west south, and east.

Meantime, while Israel continues in obstinate unbelief, it is our privilege and responsibility to preach the Gospel of the grace of God to every creature. Are we whole-heartedly in this blessed service?

There is an allusion to the molten sea in Revelation 4.6; but what John saw in heaven was not a sea of water, but "a sea of glass like unto crystal." The purity of heaven is fixed; no more shall we need to "cleanse ourselves" as we are exhorted in 2 Corinthians 7.1.

Ten Bases and Ten Lavers

Ten bases of brass, with wheels, were made upon which ten lavers rested. Remarkably, more is said about the bases than about the lavers. This would scarcely be man's method of writing; but the Holy Spirit's ways are always divinely wise whether we understand them or not. The bases and lavers are described at some length in 1 Kings 7.27-39; but their use is told us in 2 Chronicles 4.6. "Such things as they offered for the burnt-offering they washed in them; but the sea was for the priests to wash in." Every sacrifice that was brought to the altar spoke to God of Christ. This being so, they must be absolutely clean. When Noah came out of the ark, he "builded an altar unto Jehovah, and took of every clean beast, and of every clean fowl, and offered burnt-offerings upon the altar" (Gen. 8.20). This action showed that he had been taught of God. When the leper was to be cleansed, a very lowly offering was prescribed - two sparrows; but it was stipulated that they should be clean

(Lev. 14.4). Thus would God teach us pictorially lessons concerning His Holy One:

> *"He did no sin" (1 Peter 2.22).*
> *"He knew no sin" (2 Cor. 5.21).*
> *"In Him is no sin" (1 John 3.5).*

Well may we sing:-

> *"Thy life was pure without a spot,*
> *And all Thy nature clean."*

His spotlessness was necessary for His sacrifice. Prove one flaw in the Christ of God, and the blood of His cross loses its value, and nothing can save us from the damnation of Hell.

"Which of you convinceth Me of sin?" was His challenge soon after His pointed words to the accusers of an adulterous woman, "He that is without sin among you, let him first cast a stone at her" (John 8.7-46). Men felt constrained to say of Him, "He hath done all things well" (Mark 7.37); and the Father said immeasurably more when twice He opened the heavens, and testified, "This is My beloved Son, in whom I am well pleased" (Matt, 3.17; 17.5).

Ten Lampstands

The number ten and its multiples has a large place in the Temple arrangements. The Temple itself was 60 cubits long, 30 cubits broad, and 30 cubits high; the Oracle was 20 cubits long, 20 cubits broad, and 20 cubits high; and the porch in front of the house was 20 cubits long, 20 cubits high, and 10 cubits broad. Amongst the furnishings we find ten brazen lavers set upon ten bases; ten candlesticks (lampstands) of gold (1 Kings 7.49); ten tables of gold, and hundred golden bowls for sprinkling (2 Chron. 4.8).

Numbers in Scripture have meaning. Ten is the number of

responsibility, evidenced in the ten commandments of the Law. The prominence of ten in Solomon's Temple is thus a reminder that everything was being set up on the ground of responsibility, and that the continuance of that marvellous system of glory and blessing depended upon the faithfulness of king and people. "The candlesticks of pure gold, five on the right side, five on the left, before the Oracle, with the flowers, and the lamps, and the tongs of gold" (1 Kings 7.49). The Tabernacle had but one lampstand, and for the Millennial Temple none at all are mentioned. The ten in Solomon's temple are therefore particularly suggestive. Would the royal house of David be true to its trust as witness for God amongst the nations? Alas, for the answer! Yet the forbearance of God was wonderful. When in His anger He told Solomon that his kingdom should be rent, He added, "but I will give one tribe to thy son for David my servant's sake, and for Jerusalem's sake which I have chosen" (1 Kings 11.13). To Jeroboam He said that David His servant was to have a lamp always before Him in Jerusalem, "the city which I have chosen Me to put My name there" (1 Kings 11.36). When recording the unfaithfulness of Abijam, Solomon's grandson, God said, "Nevertheless for David's sake did Jehovah his God give him a lamp in Jerusalem, to set up his son after him, and to establish Jerusalem" (1 Kings 15.4).

In 2 King 17, the whole situation as regards Israel is divinely summed up. After 260 years of separate national existence under nineteen kings, all evil, Jehovah gave the ten tribes up to the Assyrian oppressor. "Jehovah was very angry with Israel and removed them out of His sight: there was none left but Judah only" (verse 18). Judah learned no lesson from the ruin of their brethren. For 130 years longer Jehovah bore with their evil ways, and finally gave them into the hands of Nebuchadnezzar. "Judah kept not the commandments of Jehovah their God, but walked in the statues of Israel, which they made. And Jehovah rejected all the seed of Israel, and afflicted them, and delivered them into the hands of spoilers, until He had cast them out of His sight" (verses 19-20). The "throne of Jehovah," established in Jerusalem, was overthrown; and David's lamp was extinguished. All is lost on the ground of responsibility, but grace will yet more than restore what Solomon and Israel so foolishly threw away. God has pledged Himself that David shall never want a man to sit upon his throne. Christ is the fulfilment of this. Rejected by the people in their blindness at His first coming, He now sits at Jehovah's right hand in heaven. "Sit Thou," is God's word to Him to-day; "Rule Thou" will be his mandate to Him shortly (Psalm 110.1-2). Until that great day Israel and the nations must continue to writhe in ever-increasing wretchedness. "The times of the Gentiles" must run on to their appointed end (Luke 21.24). Sin's wages are very terrible.

* * * * * * * * *

John in Patmos was shown seven golden lampstands (Rev. 1.3). These represented seven local Assemblies then existing; and prophetically they show us the Church as a whole from first to last. It was a testimony set up in divine righteousness, but the failure is made painfully clear. The lampstand will be removed. Christ alone is God's "faithful witness" (Rev. 1.5).

The Veil

The Oracle was shut off from the Holy Place by folding doors made of olive wood, joined to the side posts by hinges of gold. But there was also a veil in the Tabernacle, apparently hung with chains of gold (2 Chron. 3.14-16). It is noteworthy that neither the veil nor the brazen altar are mentioned in the "Kings" description of the Temple, but in the "Chronicles" account only. This is because in the earlier description the Temple is viewed primarily as the dwelling-place of God; but in the later it is rather the seat of divine government, and the place of approach for God's people. A somewhat similar distinction is found in the instructions concerning the Tabernacle. In Exodus 25.-27. 19 the manifestation of God is the great thought; thus we begin with the ark and other vessels of display. From Exodus 27.20 onwards we have the means whereby the people could have to do with God, and in those chapters we find the priesthood and the altar of incense. In the first section we have God drawing near to men, and in the second we have men drawing near to God. Let us seek grace and wisdom to "rightly divide the word of truth" (2 Tim. 2.15).

The veil was alike in both Tabernacle and Temple. Hebrews 10.20 teaches us that it typifies the flesh of Christ. A divine wonder is here. Hebrews 1. is occupied with the greatness and majesty of the Son. He has an eternal throne, and angels worship Him. Yet He took to Himself "the likeness of sinful flesh" (Rom. 8.3). He became truly man in order that He might undertake our cause. But He is nevertheless our Lord and our God (John 20.28). Not only is He the perfect and only manifestation of God to men, He is the only way of approach to God. "Through Him we have access."

No one but the priests ever saw the veil either in the Tabernacle or in the Temple. Others saw the entrance to the sacred enclosures, and they could enter through them in order to reach the altar of sacrifice; further, the people in general dare not go. When King Uzziah ventured into the Temple itself he was smitten with leprosy for his presumption (2 Chron. 26.16). Our privileges as believers in the One who has entered in the power of His own blood are truly wonderful. Not only have we been permitted to draw near to God as sinners seeking pardon (this would answer to the Israelite approaching the brazen altar); we are now worshipping priests, and may enter freely into the holiest. We not only gaze upon the veil, we pass through it. The divine action at the moment of the Saviour's death, whereby the veil of the temple "was rent in the midst" (Luke 23.45) "from top to bottom" (Matt. 27.51) signified God's rejection of that order of things which kept His people at a distance from Himself. But how persistently has Satan laboured through the centuries to enslave men to priestly orders and ritualistic observances, to the dishonour of the work of the Lord Jesus and to the damage of their souls! Every believer should be able to joyfully sing:-

> *"So near so very near to God,*
> *I cannot nearer be;*
> *For in the person of His Son*
> *I am as near as He."*

But this would raise a great outcry, and the unwanted officials might say as Demetrius of old to his fellows, "Sirs ye know that by this craft we have our wealth!" (Acts 19.25).

One verse describes the Temple Veil. "He made the veil of blue, and purple, and crimson, and fine linen, and wrought cherubim thereon" (2 Chron. 3.14). Its very existence proclaimed that "the way into the holiest was not yet made manifest" (Heb. 9.8). But it nevertheless spoke of Christ. The *blue* reminds us that He is "out of heaven," in contrast with the first man who was "out of the earth, earthy" (1 Cor. 15.47). Such is our wonderful position in relation to God that we need a heavenly Priest (Heb. 7.26). If the Aaronic priesthood existed today, it could not help a people who are nearer to God than themselves. *Purple* is suggestive of His universal dominion. Not yet is this in His hands; but we shall yet behold Him honoured and adored throughout God's wide creation. *Crimson* speaks of both suffering and glory. He who suffered here will in God's appointed time have glory here. Meanwhile, the harlot of Revelation 17. arrays herself with every mark of earthly splendour. The *fine linen* into which the colours were wrought tells of the spotlessness of Him who suffered on the tree; the *cherubim* assure us that it is He who will judge righteously for God, when the present period of grace has come to an end.

"Within the Holiest of all,
Cleansed by His precious blood,
Before the throne we prostrate fall,
And worship Thee, our God."

The Brazen Altar

As with the veil, so with the altar of Burnt Offering, the Holy Spirit gives us but one verse concerning it in the book of Chronicles. In the Book of Exodus fifteen verses are devoted to its predecessor in the tabernacle, and in Ezekiel many verses are appropriated to the altar and its service in the Millennial Temple. Solomon "made an altar of brass, twenty cubits the length thereof, and twenty cubits the breadth thereof, and ten cubits the height thereof" (2 Chron. 4.1). Here we have no description whatever of this most essential vessel. But its great size is noted. In length and breadth it was four times as large as the altar in the tabernacle. It was approximately 30 feet long, 30 feet broad, and 15 feet high! Its measurements in length and breadth exactly corresponded to the Oracle, "the most holy house" (2 Chron. 3.8), thus giving us the sweet assurance that the sacrifice of Christ is equal to all the demands of the holiness of God. What rest and peace this gives to conscience and heart!

The altar of Burnt Offering was made of brass. Bronze or copper is perhaps the correct word for the metal used. Here is a quotation from a departed friend: "Gold is the righteousness of God for drawing near where God is; brass is the righteousness of God for dealing with man's evil where man is" (W. Kelly). This being so, the vessels within the house were made of gold, and those outside - altar, molten sea, bases and lavers, were made of brass.

The brazen altar leads us in thought to "the wondrous cross on which the Lord of glory died." No vessel in the Temple compared with the altar for size. Truly, there is nothing like the cross. When the great sacrifice was drawing near, "Jesus said,

Now is the Son of Man glorified, and God is glorified in Him. If God is glorified in Him, God shall also glorify Him in Himself, and shall straightway glorify Him" (John 13.31-32). Man's side of the cross - the shame and spitting, is not in view in these words. (1) The cross was the glory of the Son of man. Perfect love and perfect obedience were expressed there. (2) God was glorified. All that He is shone out in the cross of Jesus - His righteousness, holiness, truth, grace and love. In no other way could God have thus displayed His glory. (3) As surely as the Son of man delighted to glorify God at all cost to Himself, so God delighted to glorify Him. He has not to wait for the day when He will sit upon David's throne, God "straightway" glorified Him at His own right hand in heaven.

Every sacrifice offered upon the brazen altar spoke to God of Christ. All the offerings prescribed in Leviticus 1-7. found their perfect and final answer in His death upon the tree. Calvary's cross became for Him, in His wondrous grace, the altar of sacrifice. The fire of God's judgment went forth against Him in the day of His grief, and the whole dread question of sin was settled by His sacrifice never to be raised again with those who believe in His name.

* * * * * * * * *

THE GOLDEN ALTAR, upon which incense was burnt daily (Luke 1.9), is only mentioned incidentally in the Temple instructions, no description at all being given in the three brief notices of it (1 Kings 6.22; 7.48; 2 Chron. 4.19). Yet fourteen verses are devoted to the golden altar in the Tabernacle. For the Millennial Temple, no golden altar is indicated in Ezekiel.

* * * * * * * * *

In close proximity to the altar of Burnt Offering in Solomon's Temple stood the molten sea. Atoning blood characterized the one, and water for cleansing characterized the other. This recalls two utterances from the lips of the Lord Jesus on the night of His betrayal. As He sat down with His disciples at the Supper Table, having first washed their feet, He said:-

"He that is washed (bathed) needeth not save to wash his feet, but is clean every whit" (John 13.10).

After supper, he took up, not the bason again, but the winecup, and said:-

"This is My blood of the new covenant, which is shed for many for the remission of sins" (Matt. 26.28).

The water and the blood! thus meeting our whole need as guilty before God, and also in nature unfit for His holy presence. Nothing but the blood could make expiation for our sins. Solomon's multitudinous sacrifices were not sufficient to remove even one sin (1 Kings 8.63; Heb. 10.4); but they spoke eloquently to God of the coming sacrifice of His beloved Son, by which He made an end of our sins once and for ever. In virtue of His one offering God is able to say to His people, "Your sins and iniquities will I remember no more," and we stand before Him "sanctified" and "perfected for ever" (Heb. 10.12-17).

But this applies to our guilt. More than this, we are in nature evil irremediably. The life inherited from the first fallen man is corrupt. "I know that in me (that is, in my flesh) dwelleth no good thing" (Rom. 7.18). A new life as well as pardon for sins, is necessary ere any man can dwell with God. Blessed be His name, our whole need is met in the death of Christ. He died for the sinner as well as for his sins, and faith can say "our old man has been crucified with Him" (Rom. 6.6). The Word of God brings this home with power to heart and conscience, and the believer henceforth 'lives before God in the life of the risen Christ. He "is our life" (Col. 3.4). The proof of this is seen in new tastes and aspirations. The things once loved are no longer wanted, and things once despised are the objects of deep delight. It is a moral purification - new birth. This can never be repeated. Hence the Lord's words to the impulsive Peter, who first refused to allow Him to wash his feet, and then said, "Lord, not my feet only, but also my hands and my head, He that is washed needeth not, save to wash his feet, but is clean every whit" (John 13.9-10).

Aaron and his sons on the day of their consecration were washed with water by Moses at the door of the Tabernacle (Lev. 8.6). This typified new birth, and was never repeated. Hebrews 10.22 applies the reality of this to Christians. But Aaron and his sons needed daily cleansing, and for this they had recourse to the laver. In like manner we need continual cleansing for our feet, for we walk in a sinful world, and for this there is "the washing of water by the Word" (Eph. 5.26).

The efficacy of the blood of Jesus has been applied to us by the Holy Spirit, and it abides. There is no repetition of it, for our guilt has been cancelled for ever. But the water, by means of which Christ and His great work wrought on our behalf is brought before us , is a daily and hourly necessity. Only thus can we walk with God in unclouded communion.

The Ark of the Covenant

The ark was not a distinctively Temple vessel. It was the same as was placed in the tabernacle, and which accompanied the children of Israel in all their vicissitudes. But amongst all the beautiful and costly things that Solomon made for the sanctuary of God none compared with the ark in importance. Indeed the Temple was the resting-place of the ark! Quoting the words of Psalm 132., we hear Solomon saying at the close of his great prayer at the dedication of the temple, "Now therefore arise, O Jehovah God, into Thy resting-place, Thou, and the ark of Thy strength: let Thy priests, O Jehovah God, be clothed with salvation, and let Thy saints rejoice in goodness" (2 Chron.

6.41).

The ark was the highest type of Christ in that age of types.
The shittim wood (acacia), and the gold which covered it
speaks of His person as both man and God; the mercy-seat upon
the ark speaks of His sacrifice, for the blood of the sin-offering
was always upon it. As the receptacle for the tables of the law,
righteousness was expressed by it. Grace in God has found a
way whereby transgressors can be blessed. That way is Christ
and His atoning sacrifice.

The history of the ark may be briefly stated:-

Moses placed it at the first in the Holy of Holies (Exod. 40.21).
On the march it was appointed to be carried in the centre of the
host (Num. 2.17).
Moses' strange request to Hobab caused Jehovah to send the
ark three days' journey in advance (Num. 10.33).
The ark passed through Jordan before the people (Josh. 3.11).
It was carried around the walls of Jericho on the shoulders of
the priests (Josh. 6.).
Its first abode in Canaan was Shiloh, in Ephraim's territory
(Josh. 18.1).
Having been used by Israel as a "mascot," Jehovah delivered
the ark to the Philistines (1 Sam. 4; Psalm 78.60-61).
Dagon fell before it (1 Sam. 5.), and Philistine cities were
smitten: Jehovah thus asserted His majesty amongst the
heathen.
Bethshemesh was smitten because of irreverence on the return
of the ark (1 Sam. 6.).
Kirjath-jearim, house of Abinadab, was its next halting-place
(1 Sam. 7.1).
David moved to bring the ark up to Zion, but his error in placing
it on a cart, and Uzzah's irreverence in touching it, caused it to
be carried instead to the house of Obed-Edom the Gittite (2
Sam. 6.10-11).

The report of the great blessing to the Gittite led to the ark being removed on the shoulders of the Levites to the city of David with great rejoicing (2 Sam. 6.14-19).

The ark never returned to the Tabernacle. Solomon offered sacrifices before it in 1 Kings 3.15.

When the Temple was completed, the priests put the ark into the Holy of Holies, and drew out the staves. Its travels were ended (2 Chron. 5.7).

At the destruction of Jerusalem the ark was not specifically mentioned, but the following words may be noted: "The king of Babylon. . . carried out thence all the treasures of the house of Jehovah" (2 Kings 24.13).

Amongst the sacred vessels that were restored in the days of Zerubbabel, the ark is not mentioned.

Before the captivity, in the good reign of Josiah, Jeremiah was guided to write thus of days of blessedness yet to come: "It shall come to pass, when ye be multiplied and increased in the land, in those days, saith Jehovah, they shall no more say, The ark of the covenant of Jehovah: neither shall it come to mind: neither shall they remember it; neither shall they visit it; neither shall it be done any more. At that time they shall call Jerusalem the throne of Jehovah, and all the nations shall be gathered unto it, to the name of Jehovah, to Jerusalem" (Jer. 3.16-17). There is no mention of an ark for the Millennial Temple as described in Ezekiel.

* * * * * * * * * *

Amongst the visions shown to John in Patmos we find the following: "And the temple of God was opened in heaven, and there was seen in His Temple the ark of His covenant: and there were lightnings, and voices, and thunderings, and an earthquake, and great hail" (Rev. 11.19). It was but a vision, but very sustaining to faith as assuring us of the immutability of divine counsels. In the opening verses of the same chapter we see the earthly city Jerusalem, with its Temple, at the mercy of Gentile oppressors; the concluding verse assures us that nevertheless the counsels of God stand. His ancient people are remembered in Heaven, and His covenant of grace is to be fulfilled. The world's last fearful crisis will revolve around Israel. The judgments of God will overwhelm all their enemies, and the people will emerge from their afflictions the better fitted to lead the nations. The following vision (Rev. 12.) shows us Israel in queenly splendour, adorned with all the symbols of authority-sun, moon, and stars. Satan's opposition to this divine purpose, and much more to the Christ in whom everything is centred is also shown with God's delivering power and grace.

"Scoured" Brass

If we understand 1 Kings 7.13-50 aright, Solomon personally superintended the making of all vessels of gold for the house of Jehovah, and Hiram, King of Tyre, made all the vessels of brass. Under him wrought a skilled man of the same name, "son of a woman of the daughters of Dan, and his father was a man of Tyre" (2 Chron. 2.14). The association of the Israelite and the Gentile in the two kings, and the union of both in the person of the skilled workman, reminds us again that Jehovah had Gentiles in His mind for blessing as well as His people Israel when He caused the Temple to be built. "Let not the son of the stranger, that hath joined himself to Jehovah, speak, saying, Jehovah hath utterly separated me from His people. . . . Even them will I bring to My holy mountain, and make them joyful in My house of prayer: their burnt offerings and their sacrifices shall be accepted upon thy altar; for Mine house shall be called a house of prayer for all people" (Isa. 56.3-7). How evil therefore were the zealots who assaulted Paul in Jerusalem because they supposed that he had taken Trophimus an Ephesian into the Temple area! (Acts 21.28). Our Lord's warning in Matthew 8.11 might well have been thundered into their ears.

The brazen vessels for the Temple were numerous. The

princes of Israel, before David's death, gave 18,000 talents of
brass, in addition to their contributions of gold, silver, and iron
(1 Chron. 29.7). But this was not all. "Solomon left all the
vessels unweighed, because they were exceeding many; neither
was the weight of the brass found out" (1 Kings 7.47).

We are told that "all the vessels which Hiram made to King
Solomon for the house of Jehovah were of bright brass" (1
Kings 7.45). "*Bright* brass," or, as the margin reads, "made
bright," or "scoured." A small detail not to be overlooked by
those who would learn the mind of the Spirit. Thus scouring
makes bright. Surely a parable is here! "No chastening for the
present seemeth to be joyous, but grievous: nevertheless
afterward it yieldeth the peaceable fruit of righteousness unto
them which are exercised thereby" (Heb. 12.11). There are
three ways in which chastening may be treated. We may
despise it; we may faint under it; or we may be exercised by it.
For the exercised soul there is a blessed "afterward." The
scouring has done its work. Yet we all shrink from the ordeal.
Paul, when first conscious of the thorn in his flesh, besought the
Lord to remove it. He was persistent. No immediate reply
being granted him, he besought the Lord thrice. But when the
word of the Lord came to him, the suffering man was satisfied.
"He said unto me, My grace is sufficient for thee; for My
strength is made perfect in weakness. Most gladly therefore
will I rather glory in my infirmities, that the power of Christ
may rest upon me. Therefore I take pleasure in infirmities, in
reproaches, in necessities, in persecutions, in distresses for
Christ's sake: for when I am weak, then am I strong" (2 Cor.
12.7-10). If his afflictions, which tended to reduce him to a
nullity, furnished opportunity for the power of Christ to spread
itself like a tent over him, it was enough. Christ was seen, not
Paul. This was as it should be.

God sometimes gets His best out of suffering saints. The late
G. V. Wigram said, "With a heart broken, and a will subdued,
I have given thanks for sorrows in which the iron entered into

my very soul. I say not with levity, but as before God, 'Thou knowest that I could not have lived through this and that if Thou hadst not given me grace to receive it at Thy hand, and to find that out of the eater came forth meat.'" The philosopher Bacon reminds us that "the pencil of the Holy Ghost hath laboured more to describe the afflictions of Job than the felicities of Solomon." It is noticeable also that the Spirit of God has devoted more than treble the space to the history of David than to the history of Solomon. The suffering David has left us a priceless heritage in the Book of Psalms, but it is certainly true that

> *"David's psalms had ne'er been sung,*
> *If David's heart had ne'er been wrung."*

The Spirit has recorded the locality, and the character of the ground, in which Hiram did his work. "In the plain of Jordan did the king cast them, in the clay ground between Succoth and Zarthan" (1 Kings 7.46). We are all surely living in "the clay ground" while we await the coming of the Lord Jesus; but we are being formed and fashioned by His hand, and as certainly as Hiram at the end of his labours presented to Solomon a multitude of brightly shining sacred vessels fit for the sanctuary of God, so the Holy Spirit at the end of His present gracious work will present in heavenly glory a multitude of souls meet in every way for the companionship of the First-born Son.

* * * * * * * * * *

It is painful to refer, if ever so briefly, to the after history of all that which Solomon and Hiram wrought. Only five years after Solomon's death, Shishak, King of Egypt, plundered the Temple. "He took away the treasures of the house of Jehovah, and the treasures of the king's house: he even took away all: and he took the shields of gold which Solomon had made" (1

Kings 14.26). There were probably some replacements, but the Temple was plundered more than once by unfaithful kings in order to pay tribute to Gentile Powers. In due course came the terrible day when Jehovah could no longer tolerate the evil nation, and everything was given up to destruction. With sorrow of heart the inspired historian tells us of the breaking up of the famous pillars Jachin and Boaz, the bases, the molten sea, the twelve brazen bulls, etc. - all then loaded up as "scrap" in a dismal convoy of wagons, and transported to Babylon! "The brass of all these vessels was without weight" (Jer. 52.20). Thus did "the times of the Gentiles" begin, and they are not ended yet. Israel still bleeds, and the nations of the earth find no rest. Oh, the folly of sin against God!

"Oh that My people had hearkened unto Me, and Israel had walked in My ways! I should soon have subdued their enemies, and turned My hand against their adversaries" (Psalm 81.13-14).

Bringing up the Ark

THE Temple was pre-eminently the resting-place of the ark. When the building was finished, Solomon and the people brought up from Gibeon "the Tabernacle of the congregation ("tent of meeting") with all its sacred vessels (2 Chron. 5.5). This is the last historical notice of the spiritually suggestive sanctuary which Moses built in the wilderness. None of its sacred vessels entered Solomon's Temple. With the ark it was different. It had not been in the Tabernacle since the sad days of Eli. David pitched for the ark a tent in Zion, the Tabernacle being in Gibeon. The ark was brought up from its Zion tent by Solomon and the people with all possible honour. "In it (the Temple) have I put the ark, wherein is the Covenant of Jehovah that He made with the children of Israel" (2 Chron. 6.11).

The ark was a great type of Christ. Its mercy-seat (or propitiatory) was Jehovah's throne. It was the sign of His presence in the midst of the people whom His grace had delivered from the bondage of Egypt. It was a notable day in Israel when the much-travelled ark reached its resting-place. The singers, who had served since David's institution of them in two companies, some with the Tabernacle and some with the ark (1 Chron. 16.37-42), were now united.

There are points of difference between David's removal of the ark from Kirjath-Jearim to Zion, and Solomon's removal of it into the Temple. Both were days of national rejoicing, but there was a holy enthusiasm in David that was peculiar to himself, and which was very precious to God. "David danced before Jehovah with all his might: and David was girded with a linen ephod" (2 Sam. 6.14). This was not mere fleshly excitement, but unfeigned delight in God. God was coming nearer to His servant! Michal might despise his manifestations of joy, but God estimated them at their true worth. Wholeheartedness is surely due to such a God as ours!

"I will praise Thee, O Jehovah, with my whole heart" (Psalm 9.1).

"With my whole heart have I sought thee" (Psalm 119.10).

"I cried with my whole heart; hear me, O Jehovah" (Psalm 119.145).

Thus did David delight to speak to his God. "Lord, save us all from dead decent formality in divine things; give us David's spirit!"

"There was nothing in the ark save the two tables which Moses put therein at Horeb when Jehovah made a covenant with the children of Israel, when they came out of Egypt" (2 Chron. 5.10). The ark had also contained a golden pot full of manna, and Aaron's rod that budded, as Hebrews 9.4 reminds us; but these spoke of wilderness needs which were now past. The tables of stone remained, for they formed the basis of all the laws of the kingdom. Nehemiah in his confession (chap.

9.13) acknowledged that they were "right judgments, and true laws, good statutes, and commandments." "The law is holy," says Paul the Apostle (Rom. 7.12). What a different world it would have been had the Kings of Israel and all the nations carried out its every injunction!

When the priests came out of the holy place, having drawn the staves out of the ark, the Levitical choir arrayed in white linen, took their stand at the east end of the altar of burnt-offering, and sounded with their cymbals, psalteries, and harps, and with them 120 priests blew their trumpets. The voice of praise ascended to heaven. They "praised Jehovah, saying, For He is good: for His mercy (loving-kindness) endureth for ever" (2 Chron. 5.11-13). The terms of this divinely-taught ascription of praise, found frequently in the Psalms, are a guarantee of future restoration and blessing for Israel. The people and their kings have deeply failed; but Israel's God will never fail.

But what was the meaning of all this exuberance of joy when the ark was thus placed in the Temple? To the outward eye it was but a small gold-covered chest, beside which the brazen altar looked immense. The ark was the symbol of Jehovah's presence, and He who in Moses' day accepted the Tabernacle in the wilderness and took up His abode therein was now a second time coming to dwell in the midst of His people. But faith would not confound the symbol with the reality. Solomon showed in his prayer that he had **GOD** before him that day. In the evil days of Hophni and Phinehas the people sent for the ark "that when *it* cometh among us, *it* may save us out of the hand of our enemies" (1 Sam. 4.3). We wonder not that the benighted Philistines so mistook the symbol for the reality that they trembled when they heard the Israelites shout with triumph at the sight of the ark, and said, "God is come into the camp...woe unto us!" But Israel should have known better, and God so resented their superstitious carnality that He let the sacred ark fall into the enemy's hand (Psalm 78.61). At a later date when the people cared nothing for Jehovah and His commandments, and yet gloried in their possession of sacred externals, He said, "The heaven is My throne, and the earth is My footstool; where is the house that ye build unto Me? and where is the place of My rest? For all those things have My hand made, and all those things have been, saith Jehovah: but to this man will I look, even to him that is poor and of a contrite spirit and trembleth at My word" (Isa. 66.1-2). Thus the heart of a humble man, right towards God, was a more agreeable dwelling-place for Him than Jerusalem's costly temple. Our God loves reality. Two or three humble souls who come together because they delight in Him are more to the Lord Jesus today than all the imposing ritual of Christendom. "There am I in the midst of them." But there must be reality of heart, and sensitiveness of conscience concerning His will, else the simple conventicle is no more acceptable to Him than that against which it protests. Nay, it can be even more offensive in His sight because of its high pretensions. The exercised reader would do well to read carefully Jeremiah 7.1-7.

Jehovah answered Israel's outburst of praise in a remarkable way. "The house was filled with a cloud, even the house of Jehovah, so that the priests could not stand to minister by reason of the cloud: for the glory of Jehovah had filled the house of God" (2 Chron. 5.13-14). The same thing happened to the Tabernacle, so that even Moses could not enter (Exod. 40.35). Moses, as mediator, had privileges beyond those of Aaron, but even he could not go into the sanctuary at that supreme moment. Ezekiel gives us the sorrowful history of the departure of the glory when Jehovah felt constrained in righteousness to forsake His house. Chapters 9.3; 10.4, 18; 11.23 describe the stages of its departure, as if God was most reluctant to give up His people. Chapter 10.4 tells us that "the court was filled with the brightness of Jehovah's glory," and Chapter 11.23 records that the glory-cloud paused on the mountain on the east side of the city (Olivet) before its final removal. Hear the word of Jehovah: "I will go and return to My place, till they acknowledge their offence, and seek My face: in their affliction they will seek Me early" (Hosea 5.15). What it cost the heart of Jehovah thus to deal with the people of His choice is beyond our understanding. "How shall I give thee up?. . . Mine heart is turned within me, my repentings are kindled together" (Hosea 11.8). "The Lord of all the earth" (Josh. 3.11) became as regards His governmental dealings "the God of heaven" (Dan. 2.37; Ezra 7.23). The glory-cloud returned to the land for one brief moment when our blessed Lord was upon the Mount of transfiguration, but only three men were favoured to behold it (Matt. 17.5). They testify to us that in Him God found that delight that he has never yet found in Israel. Ezekiel was not only shown the glory departing from the temple, he was also shown its return in happier days yet to come, when the repentant nation will say to the long-rejected Jesus, "Blessed is He that cometh in the name of the Lord" (Matt. 23.39). Here is Ezekiel's prophetic vision, "the glory of Jehovah came into the house (the Millennial Temple) by the way of the gate whose prospect is toward the East. . . behold, the glory of Jehovah filled the house" (Ezek. 43.4, 5; 44.2). By the way of the East it went; by the way of the East it will return.

"Thick Darkness"

When the cloud filled the Temple, Solomon made a statement which demands some attention. "Jehovah hath said that He would dwell in the thick darkness" (2 Chron. 6.1). The words recall Exodus 20.21: "Moses drew near unto the thick darkness where God was." These passages suggest to us most vividly the contrast between knowing God as Lawgiver, and as "the God and Father of our Lord Jesus Christ." Such language as Solomon used is impossible for saints today. However intimate may have been the communion of Moses and Solomon with the God of Israel, they did not know Him as the humblest believer is entitled to know Him now. God was not yet fully revealed, for the Only-begotten Son who is in the bosom of the Father had not come forth from heaven to declare Him (John 1.18). All that God is has come out in the person and sacrifice of the Lord Jesus. Accordingly, God is said to be "in the light," and Christians are in the light with Him (1 John 1.7). "God is a light" is another thing. Light is His nature. "In the light," and "in darkness" are terms which set forth His relations with men dispensationally. Peter tells us that God "hath called us out of darkness into His marvellous light" (1 Peter 2.9). We are therefore "sons of light, and sons of the day" (1 Thess. 5.5). "Ye were once darkness (says Paul), but now are ye light in the Lord: walk as children of light" (Eph. 5.8). This is practical consistency with the exceeding grace of God. 1 John 1.7 (so frequently misunderstood) is not intended to teach us how we should walk, but where. The "how" is found in the following chapter. "He that saith he abideth in Him ought himself also so to walk, even as He walked" (1 John 2.6).

Solomon next publicly "blessed the whole congregation of Israel; and all the congregation of Israel stood" (2 Chron. 6.3). Only three kings ever publicly blessed the people of God (so far as the records speak), and they were all outstanding types of Christ - Melchizedek (Gen. 14.19); David (2 Sam. 6.18); and Solomon. Then Solomon blessed Jehovah on the people's behalf. "Blessed be Jehovah, God of Israel, who hath with His hands fulfilled that which He spake to my father David" (2 Chron. 6.4-11). In all the doings of the great day of the consecration of the Temple, the high priest is never mentioned. Everything was under the direction of the king. This brings home to us the great change that took place in Jehovah's dealings with Israel when the priestly house broke down in the days of Eli. God said concerning the priest for days to come, "He shall walk before Mine anointed for ever" (1 Sam. 2.35). The priest became secondary to the king. God's King ultimately is Christ. All blessing depends upon Him, and all authority is vested in Him.

Solomon's Great Public Prayer

A KING upon his knees in public, leading the nation in humble supplication to God! Rare spectacle; but why? Kings are but men, even though their power is great. Millions may tremble before them; but what is any king in comparison with God? The haughty Nebuchadnezzar, who so insolently defied his Maker, and cast three of His faithful servants into the burning fiery furnace was brought to the lowest depths of degradation in order that he might learn his own littleness, and the greatness and majesty of God (Dan. 3.15; 4.35). This divine dealing with the first head of Gentile Imperialism was meant to be a lesson to all who might come after him. The only real difference between king and subject in the matter of prayer is this: the king needs prayer more than any man in his dominions, because of the heavy responsibilities resting upon him, for which he must some day give account to the Sovereign of the universe. All well-disposed persons should pray continually "for kings, and for all that are in authority" (1 Tim. 2.2).

God has looked down upon three delightful spectacles of kings humbly praying before Him in Jerusalem:-

(1) Solomon at the dedication of the temple, when all was well (2 Chron. vi. 13).

(2) Jehoshaphat in a day of peril from a great invasion (2 Chron. 20).

(3) Hezekiah when threatened by the blasphemous Rabshakeh, and the Assyrian hosts (Isa. 37.15).

Had these prayers practical value? Yes, a thousand times YES. It has been truly said, referring to Hezekiah, that "a king in sackcloth was more to be dreaded than a king in a coat of mail."

Solomon "stood before the altars of Jehovah in the presence

of all the congregation of Israel, and spread forth his hands: for
Solomon had made a brazen scaffold (or platform of bronze)
of five cubits long, and five cubits broad, and three cubits high,
and had set it in the midst of the court: and upon it he stood, and
kneeled down upon his knees before all the congregation of
Israel, and spread forth his hands toward heaven, and said, O
Jehovah God of Israel, there is no God like Thee in the heaven
nor in the earth" (2 Chron. 6.12-14). It would be a pleasure to
transcribe the whole of the king's comprehensive prayer, but
space forbids. It can be read without irreverent haste by anyone
in five minutes. It has been our misfortune to have to listen to
public prayers which have taken much more time than
Solomon's, but which have contained much less definite matter.
When shall we learn the lesson that we are not heard for our
"much speaking?" (Matt. 6.7). Why do we not follow the
example of the man who said, "Friend, lend me three loaves,"
and who repeated his request until his need was met? (Luke
11.5). Definiteness and persistency in prayer are divinely
commended in the Word of God.

Psalm 127. shows us how Solomon felt on the great occasion
of the dedication of the Temple. The house was indeed
finished, but only God could maintain it, and all that was
connected with it. "Except Jehovah build the house, they
labour in vain that build it, except Jehovah keep the city, the
watchman waketh but in vain." Lovely spirit of dependence
upon God!

Solomon began his prayer by acknowledging the
incomparableness of Israel's God, always faithful to His word.
He promised David that he should never want a man to sit upon
his throne, but added, "if thy children take heed to their ways."
On the ground of responsibility all is lost. David's throne has
long disappeared; his family also. Even so, David does not lack
a man to sit upon his throne. The genealogy of his true Heir is
given in Matthew 1., and before His birth the angel said to the
mother: "The Lord God will give unto Him the throne of His

father David: and He shall reign over the house of Jacob for ever: and of His kingdom there shall be no end" (Luke 1.32-33). On the Day of Pentecost Peter told his audience in Jerusalem that the promise of God to David centres in the One whom they had crucified (Acts 2.30-31). At present He sits at the right hand of God in heaven, rejected by Israel and by all; but He will yet enter triumphantly into Zion, welcomed by the heartfelt praises of His people (Psalm 118.26).

Solomon felt that it was wonderful that God should condescend to dwell with men upon earth. "Behold, the heaven and heaven of heavens cannot contain Thee: how much less this house that I have built?" (1 Kings 8.27). Solomon's Temple has gone, but a more wonderful thing has taken its place. The Church, composed of sinners drawn from amongst Jews and Gentiles, is now His Temple (1 Cor. 3.16); His house (1 Tim. 3.15); His habitation (Eph. 2.22). No mere glory cloud fills this; the Holy Spirit has come from heaven to form the building and to take up His abode therein. Every believer in Jesus is a "living stone" in God's "spiritual house" (1 Peter 2.5). Privilege and blessing too immense to be described in words; but Satan has laboured from the beginning to rob God's saints of the realisation and joy of it. The various brands of clergy which have crippled the spiritual life of the Church through the centuries would never have come into existence had the abiding presence of the Spirit of God been held in living faith. But to the end He suffices for every real need, and humble waiting upon Him will always reap a rich reward.

However favoured and glorious Solomon might be, Solomon was not Christ. The contrast between the prayers in 1 Kings 8. and John 17. is great. Both prayers were uttered in Jerusalem. Although surrounded by magnificence, and possessed of wisdom and power without precedent, Solomon felt that stability had not yet come. Hence his prayer is full of anticipations of trouble. No such sentiments will be present in the mind of Solomon's greater Son when He takes the throne. Knowing to some extent the possibilities of poor flesh, Solomon used the word "forgive" before mentioning any specific evil (verse 30). The probable needs and troubles of the future are then stated:-

(1) Personal trespasses (verse 31-32).
(2) Military defeat (verses 33-34).
(3) Drought (verses 35-36).
(4) Famine, pestilence, etc. (verses 37-40).
(5) Danger in war (verses 44-45).
(6) Captivity in a strange land (verses 46-50).

In the midst of these forebodings of disaster the king prayed for the stranger from afar who might hear of Jehovah's great name, and come to His house in search of blessing. The Queen of Sheba and the Ethiopian eunuch are examples of this; but with this difference: the Queen got the blessing *in* Jerusalem, for all was in divine order in her day; the eunuch got the blessing *going away from* Jerusalem, the Temple being then an empty shell, the Christ of God having been rejected.

Jerusalem was Jehovah's earthly centre, hence Solomon requested that every prayer directed towards the city and sanctuary might be graciously accepted by God. Daniel remembered this in his captivity. "His windows being open in his chamber toward Jerusalem, he kneeled upon his knees three times a day, and prayed, and gave thanks before his God" (Dan. 6.10). Here again we note a difference between Solomon and Daniel. Solomon said of Israel, "they be Thy people, and Thine inheritance" (1 Kings 8.51); but when Daniel said, "Thy city and Thy people" he was gently corrected by the angel, "*thy* people and *thy* holy city" (Dan. 9.19-24). The solemn "Lo-ammi" sentence having gone forth, Daniel's people were no longer the people of God (Hosea 1.9). The link of relationship must continue broken until Israel lies low in humble repentance at the feet of the long-rejected Messiah.

In the "Chronicles" account there is an important addition to

Solomon's prayer. "Now therefore arise, O Jehovah God, into Thy resting-place, Thou and the ark of Thy strength: let Thy priests, O Jehovah God, be clothed with salvation, and let Thy saints rejoice in goodness. O Jehovah God, turn not away the face of Thine anointed: remember the mercies of David Thy servant" (2 Chron. 6.41-42). Solomon had Psalm 132. in mind as thus he concluded his prayer. The full and final blessing of Israel is in view in that Psalm, which Christ alone can bring in. This seems more suitably quoted in "Chronicles" than in "Kings," for the later record is more typical than the former.

Solomon rose from his knees, and "stood and blessed all the congregation of Israel with a loud voice" (1 Kings 8.54-61). He finished by exhorting the people: "Let your heart be perfect with Jehovah your God, to walk in His statutes, and to keep His commandments, as at this day." Everything thus depended for the time being upon the faithfulness of King and people. This being so, Solomon was led to refer, not to the promises made by Jehovah to Abraham, Isaac, and Jacob, but to those made to Moses at the time of the great deliverance from Egypt. The divine promises to Abraham, Isaac, and Jacob, which contemplate full and final blessing for Israel and for "all the families of the earth," await the coming of our Lord Jesus Christ for their fulfilment.

The Feast of Tabernacles

SOLOMON'S prayer brought an immediate acknowledgment from God. "Fire came down from heaven and consumed the burnt offering and the sacrifices: and the glory of Jehovah filled the house." This public acceptance of the sacrifices caused the whole congregation to bow low in worship, and they celebrated in song the eternal loving-kindness of their God (2 Chron. 7.1-3). Our realisation of the blessed fact that God has accepted Christ and His offering on our behalf stirs our affections, and fills our lips with praise. Our worship and praise exceeds in spiritual intelligence anything that was possible for the people of God in the age of types and shadows.

Days of religious festival followed the dedication of the temple. From North to South of the land the people threw their whole heart into it. Alas, for the contrast in hypocritical Christendom! Days of cessation from labour bearing religious names are too commonly used for more fleshly indulgence than usual! The days described in 1 Kings 8.62-66 were a bright foreshadowing of the glory, prosperity and joy that will be enjoyed by Israel (and not by Israel only) when the KING comes. As the people commenced, so they might have continued had they paid heed to the commandments of their God. Their whole course might have been prosperous and blessed unto this day. Not many years after their joyous feasts the most precious things of Jehovah's house were being transported to Egypt as spoils of war (1 Kings 14.26). Dismal sight for angels to look down upon!

The Temple was commenced in the spring of Solomon's fourth year, and was finished in the autumn of seven years later. There was order in this, as we shall see. Israel's feasts (more correctly "appointed seasons," for the Day of Atonement was no feast) are described in Leviticus 23. They were in two main divisions. We may call them the Spring feasts and the Autumn feasts. Those appointed for the Spring were:-

(1) The Passover, with its accompanying days of unleavened bread.

(2) The Sheaf of First-fruits.

(3) Pentecost, with its "new meal offering" of two wave loaves.

These have already received their fulfilment in the ways of God. The Lamb has indeed been sacrificed (1 Cor. 5.7); the Sheaf has been waved before God in the person of the risen Christ (1 Cor. 15.20), and the Pentecostal loaves are seen today in the Christian company. We are now God's witnesses in the earth.

Israel's Autumn feasts were held in the seventh month, corresponding to the British October. They were:-

(1) The blowing of Trumpets on the first day.

(2) The Day of Atonement on the tenth day.

(3) The Feast of Tabernacles from the fifteenth to the twenty-second day.

These await their fulfilment at the end of the age. Israel's tribes will yet hear the trumpet-blast that will call them back to the land of their fathers (Isa. 27.13; Matt. 24.31); there will be wrought in their souls solemn appreciation of the atoning sacrifice of Christ (Zech. 12.10; Isa. 53.5); and the joy and blessing of the Millennial Kingdom will follow in the goodness of God.

Twice seven days were kept by Solomon and his people. They commenced with the dedication of the altar of burnt offering. The sacrifices of that day almost stagger the imagination - 22,000 oxen and 120,000 sheep! Although the altar was very large, it did not suffice for sacrifices so numerous. Accordingly "the king did hallow the middle of the court that was before the house of Jehovah," and there the animals were slain and burnt. Yet we read in Hebrews 10.4, "It is not possible that the blood of bulls and of goats should take away sins." Oh, the value of the one offering of the Lord Jesus! On a single day, by the offering up of Himself, He settled the whole dread question of our sins once and for ever. "By one offering He hath perfected for ever them that are sanctified" (Heb. 10.14). "No more conscience of sins" is our happy experience. We are now God's worshippers purged once for all (Heb. 10.2). Only God knows the greatness of the Person and the preciousness of the blood which has wrought this for us. But the blessing is ours.

The words "a very great congregation" in 2 Chronicles 7.8 reminds us of Psalm 22.25. That precious Psalm, which describes our Lord's experiences as the Sin-offering in verses 1-20, also speaks in its concluding verse of the far-reaching results of His sacrifice. Kingdom-bliss is in view in verse 25 - "My praise shall be of Thee in the great congregation." Earth's long rejected Sovereign will return to Zion, and in the midst of Israel and of many nations, all at last at rest in peace, He will lead the song of praise to His God. Earth's potentates, then willingly subject to Him, will form the choir: "All the kings of the earth shall praise Thee, O Jehovah, when they hear the words of thy mouth. Yea, they shall sing of the ways of Jehovah: for great is the glory of Jehovah" (Psalm 138.4-5). Meantime the Lord Jesus has His Assembly. "My Assembly," said He in Matthew 16.18. Verse 22 of Psalm 22. is quoted by the Holy Spirit in Hebrews 2.12, and applied to the present time. "I will declare Thy name unto My brethren, in the midst of the Assembly will I sing praise unto Thee." It is but a "little flock" (Luke 12.32) when compared with the great congregation of the Kingdom-age; but the Assembly is all that He has during this period of His rejection, and it constitutes His present joy. How far do our hearts enter into this?

In the joy, or perhaps excitement, of those stirring days, Solomon and the people did not keep the feast of tabernacles quite scripturally. Leviticus 23. is explicit that on the first day of the annual feast they were to make for themselves booths of palm trees, etc. "Ye shall dwell in booths: that your generations may know that I made the children of Israel to dwell in booths, when I brought them out of the land of Egypt." This was apparently overlooked, for we read in Nehemiah 8.17 that the returned remnant from Babylon "made booths and sat under the booths: for since the days of Jeshua the son of Nun unto that day had not the children of Israel done so." Nehemiah was thus more attentive to the written Word than the great king Solomon with all his wisdom!

But our God is very merciful to those whose hearts are right towards Him, even though they fail to act strictly according to His truth. But inadvertencies in the holy things must not be regarded lightly when they become known (Lev. 5.15). Hezekiah prayed for those in his day who "had not cleansed themselves yet did eat the Passover otherwise than it was written" (2 Chron. 30.18). It is interesting to observe that in these great religious movements, both in the days of Solomon and of Hezekiah, the High Priest is not mentioned. The king led and acted, suggestive of the coming One who "shall sit and rule upon His throne: and He shall be a priest upon His throne" (Zech. 6.13).

Everything earthly comes to an end - even the Millennial Kingdom has a time limit, and "on the eight day (Solomon) sent the people away: and they blessed the king, and went unto their tents joyful and glad of heart for all the goodness that Jehovah had done for David His servant, and for Israel His people" (1 King 8.66). "Seven days and seven days, even fourteen days," yet the whole feast concluded "on the eighth day!" Typically , "the eighth day" is Eternity, for the bliss and glory of the millennial age is but the vestibule into the kingdom which will know no end. This was the day when the rejected Messiah stood in Solomon's city and cried, "If any man thirst, let him come unto Me and drink" (John 7.37). The ritual of the Feast of Tabernacles, all pointing to Himself, was in full swing, but HE was unwanted. It was true then, and it is true still, that hearts which cannot be satisfied with religious ceremonials can find full satisfaction and rest in Christ.

But neither in Solomon's day nor in the greater day of the Lord Jesus, did the people know the time of their visitation. They soon forsook the God of the Temple and served other gods; and when the God of the Temple visited them in love they cast Him out and crucified Him. Need we wonder at Israel's anguish and at the sufferings of all the nations? The end is not yet. The evil must be traced to its very root, and judged there, ere the blessing of God can again be enjoyed.

Jehovah Speaks Again

" **J**ehovah appeared to Solomon the second time, as He had appeared unto him at Gibeon" (1 Kings 9. 2). It is good to hear the voice of God. But the contrast between Jehovah speaking to Solomon at Gibeon and now in Jerusalem is great. At Gibeon Jehovah said, "Ask what I shall give thee," and the young king's answer was a real delight. But several years had passed - years of unparalleled prosperity in the goodness of God, and the Temple was now in being. Israel's blessing was therefore complete. Now Jehovah speaks solemnly to His servant about his responsibility. His prayer and supplication had been heard, and the house that he had built was now the acknowledged dwelling-place of Jehovah. "Mine eyes and My heart shall be there continually" - wonderful divine pledge! Solomon's Temple has long been destroyed; other structures have succeeded it; but Haggai 2.9 teaches us that in God's sight the house has been one throughout. "The latter glory of this house shall be greater than of the former, saith Jehovah of hosts: and in this place I will give peace" (R.V.). In the same chapter we read, "Who is left among you that saw this house in her first glory?" Compare Ezra 5.11. Even the Temple that was built by Herod for his own aggrandisement was called by the Lord Jesus "My Father's house" (John 2.16). It is perhaps more remarkable that the Temple in which the Man of Sin will sit is called "the Temple of God" in 2 Thessalonians 2.4 and Revelation 11.1.

Jehovah's answer to Solomon's prayer is given at greater

length in 2 Chronicles 7. than in 1 Kings 9. First, He graciously promised to hear the supplication of His people in times of trouble. Then He renewed His pledge that David should never want a man to sit upon the throne of Israel; but He pointedly added that this was no guarantee to the line of Solomon. That line has wholly disappeared, but Christ is God's resource. Men indeed crucified the One whom they hailed as "Son of David" (Matt. 21. 9); but God raised Him from amongst the dead. He came of the Nathan branch of David's royal house (Luke 3.31). It will be a great day for Israel when they learn in the school of affliction that all their hopes are centred in Him.

This divine communication shows clearly how everything from that moment depended upon the king. "As for *thee*, if thou wilt walk before Me, as David thy father walked. . . then will I establish the throne of thy kingdom. . . but if ye turn away and forsake My statues and My commandments. . . then will I pluck *them* by the roots out of My land, which I have given them." The subsequent history of Solomon is the more terrible as we contemplate these plain words. He should have realised that his departure from God would wreck the whole magnificent order of things which surrounded him. His foolish son Rehoboam did not help matters. Several of Solomon's successors were pious men, and God graciously granted revivals in their time; but others of his line - notably Ahaz, Manasseh, and Zedekiah, were the vilest of the vile, and they filled Judah's cup of iniquity to the uttermost. Josiah was the last king that was worth anything to the nation, and he foolishly threw away his life at the age of thirty-nine in a quarrel which belonged not to him (2 Chron. 35.20). Not long after, the princes of the royal house were eunuchs in the palace of the king of Babylon, and "our holy and our beautiful house, where our fathers praised Thee, is burned up with fire: and all our precious things are laid waste" (Isa. 64.11). These calamities were set before the people as far back as the days of Moses, and in due time they came to pass (Lev. 26; Deut. 28.29-30). Passers by who might enquire as to the cause of the ruin would be told: "Because they forsook Jehovah their God, who brought forth their fathers from the land of Egypt, and have taken hold upon other gods, and have worshipped and served them: therefore hath Jehovah brought upon them all this evil" (1 Kings 9.9).

The Lamentations of Jeremiah should be read at this point. There we have one who entered deeply into the mind of God pouring out his bitter grief for the ruin of His people. For Israel's captivity and desolation was no ordinary incident in the sorrowful history of the nations. The tragedy of Israel is the tragedy of the world; thereby the world's deliverance and blessing is held up, and has become impossible until the appearing of the Lord Jesus. Alas, the world , although at this time is in the deepest distress, does not want Him yet!

"I made me great works"

T HREE Scripture books have come down to us from the pen of king Solomon - Proverbs, Ecclesiastes, and the Song of Songs. The character of their contents suggests that these books were written at different periods in his life. The ardent language of the Song, describing the love of Bridegroom and Bride - Christ and Israel at the last, points to Solomon's early days when his spiritual affections were alert towards God; Proverbs was probably written in the days of his maturity; and Ecclesiastes, with its language of chastened disappointment, was almost certainly Solomon's latest effort. The Spirit of God led him to record his painful experiences when in search of "good under the sun" for the warning of men in all ages who might be disposed to tread the same path.

Solomon tells us in his own words of the many public works, in which he interested himself. Houses, vineyards, gardens, orchards, etc. - never had the nation seen the like! "Whatsoever mine eyes desired I kept not from them." But there was no satisfaction for his heart! "I looked on all the works that mine hands had wrought, and on all the labour that I had laboured to do: and behold all was vanity and vexation of spirit, and there was no profit under the sun" (Eccles. 2.4-11). The Amorites, Hittites, Perizzites, etc., that were left in the land were pressed into service (1 Kings 9.20-21). New cities were built, and others were rebuilt (1 Kings 9.17-19). But all this meant heavy taxation. In due course the people groaned under the burden, while Solomon groaned with heart-disappointment. It was probably the load of taxation that made the people appeal to Rehoboam to make their service less grievous and their yoke less heavy (1 Kings 12.4). Men will not thus complain when the Lord reigns in Zion. His glory will far exceed that of Solomon, but it will be as true then as now, "My yoke is easy, and My burden is light" (Matt. 11.30). Why do not the burdened nations of the earth join with us in the cry, "Come, Lord Jesus?" (Rev. 22.20).

Next to the Temple, Solomon's most important building was the house of the forest of Lebanon. This was set up in Jerusalem, but was erected with materials brought down from Lebanon. This house was much larger than the Temple. The latter was 60 cubits long by 20 cubits broad; the house of the forest of Lebanon was 100 cubits long by 50 cubits broad. Both were 30 cubits high. In this great building was kept Solomon's 300 shields of beaten gold (spoil for the Egyptians in the days of Rehoboam); and all the vessels therein "were of pure gold; none were of silver; it was nothing accounted of in the days of Solomon" (1 Kings 10.17-21). "Then he made a porch for the throne where he might judge, even the porch of judgment" (chap. 7.7). This suggests the righteous administration of our Lord Jesus in the great Kingdom-age.

The use of the number six in the description of Solomon's glories is noticeable. His ivory throne had six steps; his importation of gold in a single year was 666 talents; 600 shekels of gold were used in each of his 200 targets; and "a chariot came up and went out of Egypt for 600 shekels of silver" (1 Kings 10.14, 16, 19, 29). Six is the number of man, and is expressive of incompleteness and imperfection. The super-man of the last days who will excite the admiration of the world has 666 for the number of his name (Rev. 13.18). Seven signifies completeness and perfection, but this can never be experienced on earth until the Man of God's eternal choice comes forth in His might.

The word "profit" occurs several times in the Book of Ecclesiastes. As the disappointed monarch looked back over the many occupations of his life, he says wearily, "Behold, all was vanity and vexation of spirit, and there was no profit under the sun" (Eccles. 2.11). The Lord Jesus has ruled that if a man should gain the whole world, and lose his own soul, he would not be profited (Matt. 16.26). "But godliness with contentment is great gain" (1 Tim . 6.6). The man who penned these words found more than contentment - he found satisfaction, in Christ. In his early days he gloried in his fleshly advantages, which were neither few nor small. "But what things were gain to me, those I counted loss for Christ" (Phil. 3.7). The knowledge of the Man in the glory of God, who first descended into the lowest depths for his salvation; the knowledge, too, that the place He has taken on high He has taken on behalf of His own, who are destined to be for ever with Him and like Him there, spoiled Paul for everything here. He counted all things loss, and mere offal in the light of Christ glorified. The things that appealed to Solomon - gold, buildings, women, etc., the abundance and combination of which were ultimately his undoing, had no appeal to the Apostle. Poor he might be, persecuted and despised, but he delighted to say, "To me to live is Christ" (Phil. 1.21). Let Paul be our model, not Solomon.

The Queen of Sheba

"**K**INGS and Queens have doubtless visited one another frequently from the beginning of national history. In days when rulers had absolute authority, such visits usually had political significance. Alliances and treaties were thus planned which had far-reaching results. But the visit of the Queen of Sheba to Solomon was of a spiritual character. In her distant land she heard of Jehovah, the God of Israel, and her heart was attracted. She desired to learn more about Him from His servant who then reigned in Jerusalem. Serious questions exercised her heart, which none around her could answer; and she rightly felt that Solomon, with the wisdom given him by God, could help her. Thus she undertook the journey, and earned thereby the public commendation of the Lord Jesus a thousand years later. It is not absolutely certain just where her dominions lay, but it was probably in Southern Arabia in the regions settled by the descendants of Joktan of the line of Shem (Gen. 10.28).

This Queen's visit was the first answer to Solomon's prayer. In 1 Kings 8.41-43 he besought God to take notice of the stranger who was not of His people Israel who might come to His house from a far country for His name's sake. The Holy Spirit expressly records that it was "concerning the name of Jehovah" the Queen of Sheba consulted king Solomon (1 Kings 10.1). Blessed be God, He has always had true sheep outside the fold, and some notable examples are shown us in the Word - the Queen of Sheba, Ittai the Gittite, Ebed-Melech the Ethiopian, etc. Whatever His dispensational dealings, and these in that age were with Israel, there has always been room in His great heart for those who wanted Him, wherever and whatever they might be.

What the Queen's "hard questions" were we know not, but they were all answered in divine wisdom. The woman of

Sychar referred to the anxious problems of her own day when she said, "I know that Messiah cometh: when He is come, He will tell us all things" (John 4.25). How little she realized that she was actually conversing with the promised One! "I that speak unto thee am He." We cannot now speak face to face with Him; but His voice is to be heard in the Scriptures, and there all our soul's need is perfectly met. What the Queen heard satisfied her; but what she saw overwhelmed her. She found herself in the presence of the man whom God had exalted; she beheld his glory and majesty; she observed the dignity and happiness of those who served him; and there was no more spirit in her. In like manner our need drew us to the Christ of God, and His revelations of grace set our consciences at rest, and settled all our problems; then, being no longer harassed with a sense of need and danger, we were free to contemplate Himself. He is God's glorified Man, the One who finished the work He gave Him to do, the centre of His counsels of grace, Head of His body the Church, and of God's "universe of bliss." Stephen was so exhilarated by the sight of His present glory that he was strengthened to die in triumph; Paul was so filled and delighted with the same sight that he was strengthened to live, serve, and suffer for His name's sake. Do we not sometimes sing:-

> *"O fix our earnest gaze,*
> *So wholly, Lord, on Thee,*
> *That with Thy beauty occupied,*
> *We elsewhere none may see."*

How far do our hearts go with our words?

If dignity and joy marked those who surrounded Solomon, what shall we say of the portion of those who are identified with the exalted Christ? They (we) are the aristocracy of the universe, blessed beyond all present conception, and we shall ere long be displayed in glory in His company, to the wonder of all beholders (2 Thess. 1.10).

The Queen of Sheba perceived that it was love that prompted Jehovah to give Israel such a king. "Blessed be Jehovah thy God, which delighted in thee, to set thee on the throne of Israel, because Jehovah loved Israel for ever, therefore made He thee king, to do judgment and justice" (1 Kings 10.9). The same love has provided us with a wonderful Saviour and glorious Head, and blessed us with every spiritual blessing in the heavenlies in Him. Every favour that we now enjoy, and all that awaits us in "God's eternal day," is the fruit of His great heart of love.

Our blessed Lord put together two Old Testament characters as a testimony to the unbelieving generation around Him - Jonah and the Queen of Sheba. The preaching of Jonah was heeded by the heathen Ninevites; *His* preaching was rejected. The Queen of Sheba came a long way to hear the wisdom of a *servant* of God; the men around the Speaker were unwilling to listen to the wisdom of the *Son* of God. No toilsome journey was necessary in their case; the Eternal Son had come from Heaven into their very streets. The rejection of Him, greater than Jonah, and greater than Solomon, is the ruin of men. "He that believeth on Him is not condemned: but he that believeth not is condemned already, because he hath not believed in the name of the Only-Begotten Son of God" (John 3.18).

Horses: Gold: Wives

WHILE Israel was yet in the wilderness, Jehovah anticipated the time when the people would have a king, and He caused instructions and warnings to be written for his guidance. The king was commanded to write out for himself a copy of divine law; and he was to read therein daily that he might learn to fear Jehovah and be in all things an example to his subjects whom he must always regard as "his brethren." Israel being the special people of God must not be ruled after the pattern of Oriental despots. The King was warned not to multiply horses to himself, nor wives, nor gold (Deut. 17.14-20). In all these particulars Solomon signally failed. As the years passed, the childlike simplicity which marked him at the beginning of his reign (1 Kings 3.) faded away, and he became important and self-willed. Have we not seen something like it in the Church of God? The prosperity so graciously granted to Solomon was too much for his slender faith. The invisible and the eternal were never to him what they were to his father; but then he never had his father's training in the school of affliction. The thought is humiliating that we need affliction and sorrow to keep us right.

Solomon's Egyptian wife may have suggested horses to Solomon, for her father's kingdom appears to have been a land of horses (Isa. 31.3). In David's day we read of mules and asses; but these humble animals seem to have had no place with Solomon, if we except the day when he rode upon David's mule to be anointed at Gihon (1 Kings 1.38). Solomon himself tells us in Proverbs 21.31 that "the horse is prepared for the day of battle"; and he adds, what he afterwards quite forgot, "but safety is of Jehovah." Horses were thus used in his time for military purposes, oxen being employed in agriculture (1 Kings 19.19); but David wrote before Solomon began to reign, "A horse is a vain thing for safety, neither shall he deliver any by his great strength" (Psalm 33.17), and again, Jehovah "delighteth not in the strength of the horse" (Psalm 147.10). In days of peril Jehovah is worth more to His people than regiments of cavalry, and concerning the enemies of His own, "at thy rebuke, O God of Jacob, the chariot and horse are cast into a dead sleep" (Psalm 76.6).

But Solomon gradually drifted away from these wholesome truths. Let us beware of drifting away from what we have learned from God. The painful repetition of the words "Know ye not?" in Paul's first letter to the Corinthians should suffice to bring home to our hearts the danger of doing so.

Solomon appears to have established a considerable business in horse-dealing. "The exportation of horses that Solomon had was from Egypt: a caravan of the king's merchants fetched a drove at a price" (1 Kings 10.28-J.N.D.). The next verse tells us that he sold horses to the kings of the Hittites and of Syria. This trading may have been profitable, but Jehovah was not pleased with His servant for it. What a testimony to the heathen around, who should have learned from him that to trust in God is better than to trust in horses!

When Israel entered Canaan which was full of horses and chariots, Jehovah said, "Thou shalt hough their horses, and burn their chariots with fire" (Josh. 11.6), for Israel's God objected to the methods of the nations being employed in His work. His people's confidence must be in Himself alone.

At one period of Solomon's life he perceived the danger of riches. "Two things have I required of Thee; deny me them not before I die. Remove far from me vanity and lies: give me neither poverty nor riches: feed me with food convenient for me: lest I be full, and deny Thee, and say, Who is Jehovah or lest I be poor, and steal, and take the name of my God in vain" (Prov. 30.7-9). As we follow the history of his reign we find the love of riches growing upon Solomon. He had fleets at sea which brought him gold and silver in abundance. Gold was so common that he "made 200 targets of beaten gold: 600 shekels of gold went to one target. And he made 300 shields of beaten gold: three pounds of gold went to one shield" (1 Kings 10.16-17). Surely these were not for use in war; just ornaments! But these costly ornaments were lost in war by Rehoboam, who in his vanity made shields of brass in their stead, and caused them to be brought out in display when he went into the house of Jehovah (1 Kings 14.25-28). Oh, the pitiful vanity of poor flesh; appearances must be kept up even after the reality has departed! Blessed contrast when God restores His people in grace! "For brass I will bring gold, and for iron I will bring silver, and for wood brass, and for stones iron: I will also make thy officers peace, and thy rulers righteousness" (Isa. 60.17). All sham will be banished, and repentant Israel will enjoy God's exceeding grace.

The exercised reader should pause here and read the last chapter of Paul's first letter to Timothy. With reference to riches, two classes are indicated; those who are not rich, but who wish to be (verses 9-12); and those who are rich already (verses 17-19). The first class are warned that the pursuit of wealth leads to temptation and a snare, and into many foolish and hurtful lusts which drown men who know not God in destruction and perdition. Such a course is unworthy of those who are in union with Christ and blessed with every spiritual blessing in the heavenlies. Money is not evil in itself, but the love of it is a root from which every evil may spring. The Apostle had observed some who, by their covetousness, had erred from the faith, and pierced themselves through with many sorrows. He who would be a man of God (and there is great need of such) must flee these things, and follow after righteousness, godliness, faith, patience, and meekness. If earthly pursuits leave no time for the cultivation of these seven divine graces all that the Christian may acquire is not gain but loss.

Those who are already rich are then wisely counselled. Mark the words "rich in this world," more correctly "in the present age." This is the time of Christ's rejection. Self-indulgence in a scene where He had no resting-place for His head, and where all His rights are still denied Him is most unsuitable for those who own Him as their Saviour and Lord. Elisha's words to the grasping Gehazi may well ring in our ears and in our hearts (2 Kings 5.26). Wealthy believers are reminded that riches are uncertain, and that their confidence should be in the living God who gives us richly all things to enjoy. These last words assure us that up to a point God would have His own enjoy His bounty. Monasticism is not Christianity. But good works must abound; with liberality should we assist the needy, "laying up for ourselves a good foundation against time to come." The unjust steward of Luke 16. is an example of this. His dishonesty our Lord did *not* approve, but He did approve his prudence. While the opportunity was with him, he used it with reference to the future; the Christian should do the same; but with this difference, the steward had before him the coming dread days of unemployment, the Christian should keep in view the judgment-seat of Christ, where all our doings will be manifested in the light of God. The passage in 1 Timothy 6.19 should be read in the Revised Version. In verse 12 we are indeed exhorted to "lay hold on eternal life"; but in verse 19 we should read "that they may lay hold on what is really life." Thus a life spent in good works and in gracious consideration for others is life indeed, in contrast with the words in 1 Timothy 5.6, "She that liveth in pleasure is dead while she liveth."

Ten times in 1 Kings 10. we meet with the word "gold." Solomon loved it. But "that which is highly esteemed among men is abomination in the sight of God" (Luke 16.15). Let us remember this in our walk in the Assembly. To flatter the rich is a great offence, and to allow men to rule simply because they have more money than their fellows is disastrous; for a spiritually minded tinker is worth more to God and to his brethren than an unspiritually minded millionaire. Even to handle the Assembly's money in Jerusalem men were looked out who were "full of the Holy Spirit and wisdom" (Acts 6.3).

Solomon's interest in horses was bad; his love of gold was dangerous; but his lust for women was a tragedy. All these things were forbidden by the God of Israel, as we have seen; but as opportunities for acquisition crowded upon him the once-wise king became increasingly reckless, and so degenerated into the greatest fool of all time. He is a beacon, set in the sacred page for the warning of men in all ages. He began badly. While yet in his teens he married an Ammonitess, and had a son - Rehoboam - before he ascended the throne. Then he took an Egyptian, and later he gathered pagan women around him in hordes. Nehemiah spoke of this when he reproved the returned remnant for their unholy alliances. "Did not Solomon king of Israel sin by these things? yet among many nations there was no king like him, who was beloved of his God, and God made him king over all Israel; nevertheless, even him did outlandish women cause to sin" (Neh. 13.26).

The contrast between the opening words of chapters 10. and 11. of the first book of Kings is deeply solemn. Chapter 10. tells us of the visit of the Queen of Sheba with her spiritual difficulties, which Solomon was enabled to clear up by the grace of God given to him. His majesty, wisdom, the Temple and the King's ascent to it, and the happiness of all his servants overwhelmed her. She acknowledged the hand of God in it all and attributed it to His love for His people Israel. "But" - terrible word! - chapter 11. tells us of Solomon's host of unholy women. drawn from Moab. Ammon, Edom, etc. - "700 wives, princesses, and 300 concubines; and his wives turned away his heart." The man who prayed so humbly to Jehovah at the dedication of the Temple became a worshipper of Ashtaroth, Milcom, and other heathen abominations. He who built the Temple for Jehovah's name sank so low as to "build a high place for Chemosh the abomination of Moab, in the hill that is before Jerusalem (Olivet), and for Molech the abomination of the children of Ammon. And likewise did he for all his strange wives, which burnt incense and sacrificed unto their gods"? Jehovah's loved Zion was girdled with all that was hateful in His sight. Jerusalem centre of spiritual light in 1 Kings 10., in chapter 11. hot-bed of the grossest idolatries! Unhappy Solomon -"How are the mighty fallen!" (2 Sam. 1.27). "And Jehovah was angry with Solomon, because his heart was turned from the Lord God of Israel, which had appeared unto him twice" (1 Kings 11.9).

Let us not read the humiliating story in vain. It is written for our learning. The companionship of a holy woman, selected under the guidance of God, is an immense help and comfort to the Christian; but the influence of an unholy woman is sufficient to wreck the spiritual life and testimony of the very best. "The head of the woman is the man" (1 Cor. 11.3), and the woman taught of God acknowledges it, and accepts the leadership of her husband; but the woman who knows not God too often rejects this, and gets control over the man. Solomon, in spite of his rich endowments, fell under this evil spell, to his own undoing, and to the ruin of his people.

Proverbs 31. - presumably written by Solomon - describes with much detail the ideal woman, whose "price is far above rubies," but he never succeeded in finding her. "One man among a thousand I have found; but a woman among all those have I not found" (Eccles. 7.28). But God could have found one for him!

Apes and Peacocks

IN the early years of his reign Solomon prized wisdom and understanding above all things, and God in His goodness responded to the desire of his heart and gave him wisdom "exceeding much." He excelled in wisdom all the men of the East and all the sages of Egypt. "He was wiser than all men. . . and his fame was in all nations round about." In consequence "they came from all peoples to hear the wisdom of Solomon, for all the kings of the earth had heard of his wisdom" (1 Kings 4.29-34). In Proverbs 3.13 he commends wisdom thus: "Happy is the man that findeth wisdom, and the man that getteth understanding." Rubies and fine gold, he tells us, are worthless in comparison. But as the material prosperity of his kingdom developed, we are told that his imports were "gold and silver, ivory, and apes and peacocks" (1 Kings 10.22). Every three years the supply of all these was maintained by ships of Tarshish. "Apes and peacocks!" For a man pre-eminent in the earth for wisdom this is a descent from the sublime to the ridiculous. We find a strange blending of things that differ in Ecclesiastes 1.17: "I gave my heart to know wisdom, and to know madness and folly." In chapter 2.12 also: "I turned myself to behold wisdom, and madness and folly." Not at the same moment, surely! First, he valued wisdom as more precious than rubies and fine gold; then he resorted to madness and folly. Apes are the synonym of folly, and peacocks of vanity. We recall J. N. Darby's well-known lines:-

> *"O Lord, alas what weakness*
> *Within myself I find;*
> *No infant's changing pleasure*
> *Is like my wandering mind."*

Beloved Christian reader, we can scarcely refrain from holding up our hands in amazement at the fickleness of Israel's great king; but what about ourselves? Wisdom such as Solomon never imagined is within our reach to-day, but do we long after it? The Apostle prayed for the Colossian saints that they "might be filled with the knowledge of His will in all wisdom and spiritual understanding" (Col. 1. 9). He had in mind the great treasure which had been entrusted to him for administration, "the wisdom of God in a mystery" (1 Cor. 2.7) - the mystery of Christ and the Church (Eph. 3.) God's greatest and grandest thoughts concerning the glory of Christ have been revealed since His rejection on earth and His return on high. What men refused Him -the kingship of the Jews - was a small thing compared with that with which the Father has invested Him. He has placed Him at the head of the universe, and - wonder of wonders - He has given Him a body to share His glory, and that body is made up of sinners saved by grace. In the great mystery of God is "hid all the treasures of wisdom and knowledge" (Col. 2.3). What value do our hearts set upon this ? Paul could not teach the mystery at Corinth because of the carnality of the believers in that city.

"Apes and peacocks" - folly and vanity! Yet Solomon desired them. We may not value these particular creatures as pets, but do we in any degree cling to things which correspond to them? We sometimes sing:-

> *"All the vain things that charm me most*
> *I sacrifice them to His blood."*

But let us consult our hearts and examine our ways. What vanities have we surrendered in response to the appeal of the precious blood? In the bird world it is the male who flaunts his splendour. The pea-hen is modest in comparison with her mate. But in the world of men and women it is the female that is in special danger. Hence the Spirit's pointed words in 1 Timothy 2.9, "That the women adorn themselves in modest apparel, with shamefacedness and sobriety (or, with modesty and discretion); not with broided hair, or gold, or pearls, or costly array; but (which becometh women professing godliness) with good works." God appreciates "the ornament of a meek and quiet spirit. In His sight it is of great price" (1 Peter 3.4). Are these instructions always obeyed by women who profess to acknowledge the Lordship of Christ? Are men absolutely immune from the ape and peacock danger? Alas, no! The writer has sat alongside an "elder" at the Lord's Supper who had carefully waxed his moustache before leaving home, and this as recently as the year 1943!

Our God hates fleshly display. When Hezekiah displayed all his treasures to the messengers of the king of Babylon (probably feeling flattered by their visit) he was told that they should all be carried to Babylon, and that his sons should be eunuchs in the King's palace (2 Kings 20.12-19).

Closing Days

I T may surprise some when we say that the records of
Solomon's forty years' reign are very scanty. It has
pleased the Holy Spirit to give us sixty-five chapters about
David, but only twenty about Solomon, and several of those are
occupied with the Temple rather than with its builder. Although
Jehovah heaped favours upon Solomon such as no other king
ever had, He never had the pleasure in him that He had in his
father David.

Solomon's reign of exaltation, glory, and prosperity had a
cloudy finish. Jehovah was faithful from first to last, but His
servant was not. We cannot help contrasting the end of this
great king with that of some others noted in the sacred pages.
Jacob, after a stormy career (occasioned by his own
crookedness), had a glorious sunset. His last days were his best.
With holy dignity he pronounced blessing upon the mightiest
potentate of that period, and with spiritual discernment he
blessed the sons of Joseph. Enoch had a most delightful finish.
"Enoch walked with God: and he was not: for God took him"
(Gen. 5.24). Elijah, after years of discouragement and peril
connected with his testimony, was carried up by a whirlwind
into heaven (2 Kings 2.).

But Solomon! David's latter-day utterances fill two long
chapters (1 Chron. 28. and 29.), and the simple faith and delight
in the things of God therein expressed is exhilarating to our
souls as we read. His "last words" as given in 2 Samuel 23.,
although very subdued in tone, breathe unbounded confidence
in the faithfulness of God. But no last words of Solomon are
recorded. We have the terse statement that "Solomon slept
with his fathers, and was buried in the city of David his father:
and Rehoboam his son reigned in his stead" (1 Kings 11.43).
More about him could be read in the writings of Nathan, Ahijah,
and Iddo (2 Chron. 9.29); but no more space is devoted to this

most faulty servant in the inspired Word. He was scarcely sixty years old when he died.

It is the end of the race that tells with us all. Happy is the man who, by the grace of God, continues to run well, and who can say like Paul at the last, "I have fought the good fight, I have finished the course, I have kept the faith" (2 Tim. 4.7).

Once more, and for the last time, Solomon heard the voice of his God. When he appeared to him in Gibeon, he said, "Ask what I shall give thee," and he was pleased with the young king's reply (1 Kings 3.); in Jerusalem He addressed him in words of encouragement and warning (1 Kings 9.); now He could only pronounce sentence upon His grossly unfaithful servant. To Jerusalem He said later with reference to her idolatries, "Thou wast insatiable" (Ezek. 16.28); the same was true of Solomon. Others selected their false gods; Solomon adopted them all. Truly, "the corruption of the best thing is the worst corruption." The kingdom of Israel should now be broken up. As a witness for God it had become worthless. During forty years David had typified Christ as the Man of war; during another forty years Solomon had typified Him as the Man of peace. Now all was over, and Israel's long night of degradation was about to commence.

"I will rend the kingdom from thee, and give it to thy servant." Yet the calamity should not happen in Solomon's time, but in the reign of his son, who by his folly proved himself as unfit to rule as his father. In mercy one tribe should be left awhile, "for David My servant's sake, and for Jerusalem's sake which I have chosen" (1 Kings 11.9-13).

"When a man's ways please Jehovah, He maketh even his enemies to be at peace with him" (Prov. 16.7). So Asa proved, and Jehoshaphat his son. Both these kings had quietness and rest round about, because they did the will of God (2 Chron. 14. 7; 15.15; 20.30). Alas, concerning Solomon we read, "Jehovah stirred up an adversary unto Solomon, Hadad the Edomite"; also, "God stirred up another adversary, Rezon the son of Eliadah" (1 Kings 11.14, 23). "With the pure Thou wilt show Thyself pure; but with the froward Thou wilt wrestle" (Psalm 18.26-margin). It is a solomn thing when God is obliged to enter into controversy with any of us, but "if we would judge ourselves, we should not be judged" (1 Cor. 11.31).

When enemies rise up against us our first appeal should be to God as to why He has permitted it. The enemies themselves may have no thought of God, but they may nevertheless be His instruments for the discipline of His people. The cruel Assyrian was the rod of Jehovah's anger with respect to Israel - "howbeit he meaneth not so" (Isa. 10.5-7). The sufferings of the Hebrew Christians, under which they were disposed to faint, were apparently due to the persecution of the ungodly; but they were also the Father's gracious chastening. "Now no chastening for the present seemeth to be joyous, but grievous; nevertheless afterward it yieldeth the peaceable fruit of righteousness to them which are exercised thereby" (Heb. 12.1-13).

Hadad and Rezin appear to have been troublesome for many years, and Solomon could have crushed them; but in his greatness and majesty he apparently despised them. Jeroboam arose later, and became a much more serious foe. He was an ambitious young man, and even aspired to the throne (1 Kings 11.37). Solomon, in forgetfulness of his own words in Proverbs 16.7, already quoted, instead of exercising his conscience before God about this antagonist, sought to slay him, after the manner of Saul with David.

David's throne is guaranteed by God, not to Solomon or to any other unfaithful creature, but to Christ. Jeremiah 33.15-17 makes this clear. "In those days, and at that time, will I cause the Branch of righteousness to grow up unto David: and He shall execute judgment and righteousness in the land. . . . For thus saith Jehovah; David shall never want a man to sit upon the throne of Israel." Instigated by Satan, Athaliah might endeavour to destroy the seed royal (2 Kings 11.1); and Rezin and Pekah might plot to replace the seed of David by the son of Tabeal (Isa. 7.6); but the purpose of God stands nevertheless.

The downfall of such a man as Solomon was a tragedy of the first magnitude, for it involved the ruin and devastation of the land and the people for three thousand years, and the deferment of deliverance and blessing for all the nations of the earth. Everything has doubtless been according to the counsel and foreknowledge of God (Acts 2.23); but this does not lessen the guilt of sinful men. Before it pleased God to subject Israel to the domination of the Gentiles, He was graciously pleased to grant occasional revivals in response to the fidelity of good kings such as Hezekiah and Josiah, but the hearts of the people were never right towards their God. Excellent kings might draw the multitude after them, but they served Jehovah "but feignedly" (Jer. 3.10).

Blessed day that is coming, when the King of His choice will return, and be welcomed by the people, then fully reconciled to God. "It shall be said in that day, Lo, this is our God; we have waited for Him, and He will save us: this is Jehovah: we have waited for Him: we will be glad and rejoice in His salvation" (Isa. 25.9).

"Thy people shall be willing in the day of Thy power" (Psalm 110.3).

"In Solomon's Porch"

A THOUSAND years have passed away, and Solomon's Temple has been superseded by another, built by a stranger. Only a remnant of Israel was in God's land, under the domination of a Gentile Power. In Solomon's porch walked One whose glory far exceeded that of the famous king, but he was unwanted and unacknowledged. He had given "many infallible proofs" that He was the long-promised

Deliverer, yet He was obliged to emphasize His dignity before
them. "I say unto you, that in this place is One greater than
the temple...behold, a greater than Solomon is here"
(Matt. 12.6, 42). Alas, blind eyes can see nothing! (Matt.
13.14). The people were already saying in their hearts, "We
will not have this man to reign over us" (Luke 19.14). The Holy
Spirit remarks, "It was Winter" (John 10.22). This describes
the condition spiritually as well as physically. When Israel is
in a better mood Summer will come, for themselves and for all
nations (Matt. 24.32-33). Then it will be said, "the Winter is
past" (Song 2.11).

After all the mighty deeds which they had seen (even the
dead raised!) the Jews came around the Lord in Solomon's
porch and said, "How long dost Thou make us to doubt? If Thou
be the Christ, tell us plainly." It was hopeless to reason with
obstinate unbelief, accordingly the Lord set them aside as
manifestly not of His sheep; but he added words concerning His
true sheep, and their security as being both in His hand and in
the Father's hand which have ministered immense comfort to
believing hearts from that moment until the present. But when
He affirmed "I and the Father are one," the Jews took up stones
to stone him, and not for the first time (John 10.22-31).

Another gathering in Solomon's porch is recorded in
Acts 3. The Son of God was no longer there, having returned
to His glory by way of the cross and the tomb; but the Holy
Spirit's voice is heard speaking through the humble
instrumentality of the fishermen Peter and John. By using in
faith the name of Jesus of Nazareth these men had healed a
cripple above forty years old who had long lain at the Beautiful
gate of the Temple begging. "As he held Peter and John, the
people ran together unto them into the porch that is called
Solomon's greatly wondering." The fishermen, by divine
authority, made one of the most important pronouncements
that afternoon that have ever been made in world. After
disclaiming all credit to themselves, they gave all the glory of

the miracle to the Name of the One, whom Israel had recently killed, but whom God had raised again from the dead. Then they told the people that if they would repent of their terrible sin and turn to God, he would send Jesus Christ back. We quote from Mr. Darby's translation: "Repent therefore and be converted, for the blotting out of your sins, so that times of refreshing may come from the presence of the Lord, and He may send Jesus Christ, who was fore-ordained for you, whom heaven indeed must receive till the times of the restoration of all things, of which God has spoken by the mouth of His holy prophets since time began" (Acts 3.19-21).

This amazing overture was in keeping with our Lord's own words concerning the barren fig-tree in Luke 13.6-9. As the dresser of the vineyard He pleaded for the condemned tree: "let it alone this year also, till I shall dig about it and dung it: and if it bear fruit, well: and if not, after that thou shalt cut it down." The opening chapters of the Book of the Acts furnish the answer to His intercession. Until the death of Stephen a fresh opportunity of blessing was granted to the guilty people; the Gospel was preached "to the Jew first" (Acts 13.46).

What a moment for this world as Peter's voice rang out in Solomon's porch! Alas, for the result! The people did not humbly and gratefully welcome it (individuals did); and their leaders were so furious that they put Peter and John into prison for daring to breathe the hated name of Jesus in Jerusalem.

What more could a long-suffering God do? He sent His Son, His well-beloved, into the world with a message of peace, and men murdered Him. Then He sent His Holy Spirit with a fresh message of peace, and with the offer to send Jesus back if they would repent; but men would have none of it. This is why Israel and the nations suffer through centuries, with no hope. God's intervention in power will end it all. When He says, "Give this man place," all pretenders will be put down, and the over-humbled Jesus will be exalted (Luke 14.9-11).